CONTENTS

BUILDING YOUR OWN GARAGE?

The answer is YES! By doing the planning and all or part of the work yourself, you can have the garage you might not otherwise be able to afford. By supplying the labor and buying materials yourself, construction costs can be significantly cut.

Framing out a garage is not difficult. Standardized materials and construction techniques make it relatively easy if you take the time to plan and work carefully. All the techniques and tips you'll need are in this book. Read it carefully from cover to cover before beginning. It will help you determine the work you can handle alone, and where a little expert help might be needed to do the job right.

You can also learn many construction basics by studying existing garages. Ask your neighbors if you can take a few minutes to review their garages before you begin planning your design.

GETTING STARTED

The first step is determining what you want your garage to do. Store your car or cars? Provide a workshop area or additional storage space? If you have two cars, consider a two-and-one-half car design. But before planning too big, remember that your lot must have sufficient space for the garage site and proper setbacks from adjacent properties, sideyards, and driveways. Local building codes often set guidelines in these areas, so check with your local municipality for any restrictions that apply to your situation.

PLANNING DRIVEWAY AND PARKING AREAS

In addition to the structure itself, you'll also want to plan your new driveway, offstreet parking, or turnaround area. The illustrations on this page are designed to give you an idea of the basic space requirements. Alter them to fit your lot, but remember that adequate driveway and parking areas will add greatly to your garage's convenience.

In most cases, short approaches to two-car garages are double-width. For longer driveways, use a single-width driveway that gradually widens to the double-door opening. Drives should be wider at curves because the back wheels make a track with a smaller radius than do the front wheels.

Construction methods for concrete driveways, walks, and parking areas are similar to those covered under slab foundations later in this guide. Local ordinances can apply to these items, so consult your local building department for specifications covering required concrete thickness, grade and slope preparations, setbacks from boundaries, and so on. In general, concrete thickness is 4" to 5". The driveways must be crowned or sloped at 2% to provide drainage. The slope of any uphill grade should not exceed 14%, and any change in grade should be as gradual as possible.

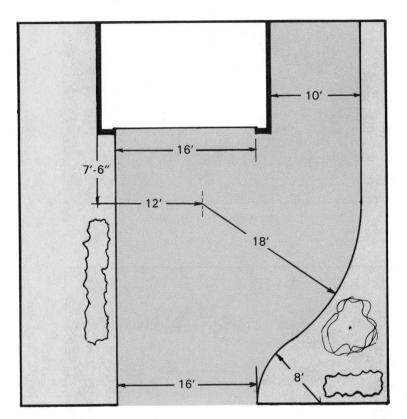

Garage With Side Parking

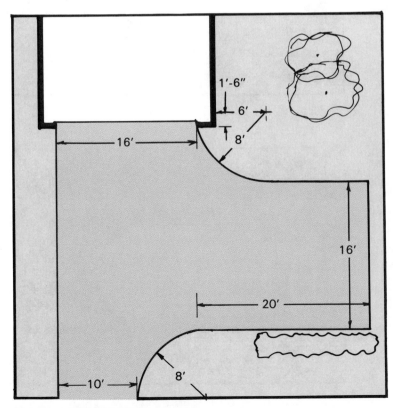

Garage, Parking, Turnaround

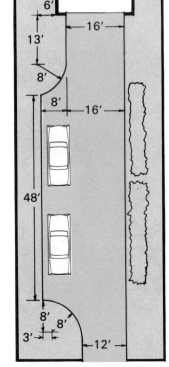

Driveway Parking Area

BASIC GARAGE DESIGNS

2 Car Hip With Storage Area

2 Car Gable

2-1/2 Car Reverse Gable With Storage

3 Car Reverse Gable

1-1/2 Car Gable With Storage Area

1 Car Reverse Gable With Storage Area and Covered Porch

WHAT SIZE GARAGE

You have a lot of latitude in deciding what kind of a garage to build. This book contains designs to help you make that decision, but remember that local zoning and building codes in most municipalities will have some effect on your final choice. There might be lot-size requirements, minimum setback regulations, height restrictions, certain building materials that cannot or must not be used. To save yourself time and future headaches, take a day or so to learn what you cannot do and what you might be required to do. In most localities, for example, at least a building permit will be required. The best place to start is at the local building and zoning code offices.

Take time to consider your possible future needs. Will a one-car garage do, or do you expect that you will need to store two cars and/or possibly a boat someday? Will you use the garage as a workshop? Is storage space in the house running short? Also consider how it will look in its proposed site. Choose a style and size that will complement its environment. Last, but certainly not least, remember your budget. Build for your needs, not your desires.

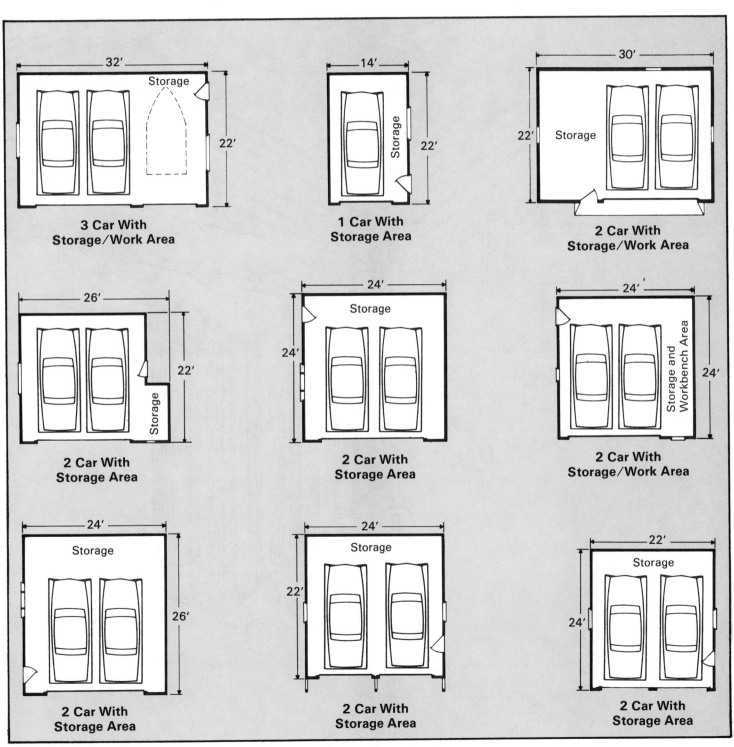

3 Car With Storage/Work Area

1 Car With Storage Area

2 Car With Storage/Work Area

2 Car With Storage Area

2 Car With Storage Area

2 Car With Storage/Work Area

2 Car With Storage Area

2 Car With Storage Area

2 Car With Storage Area

ANATOMY OF A GARAGE

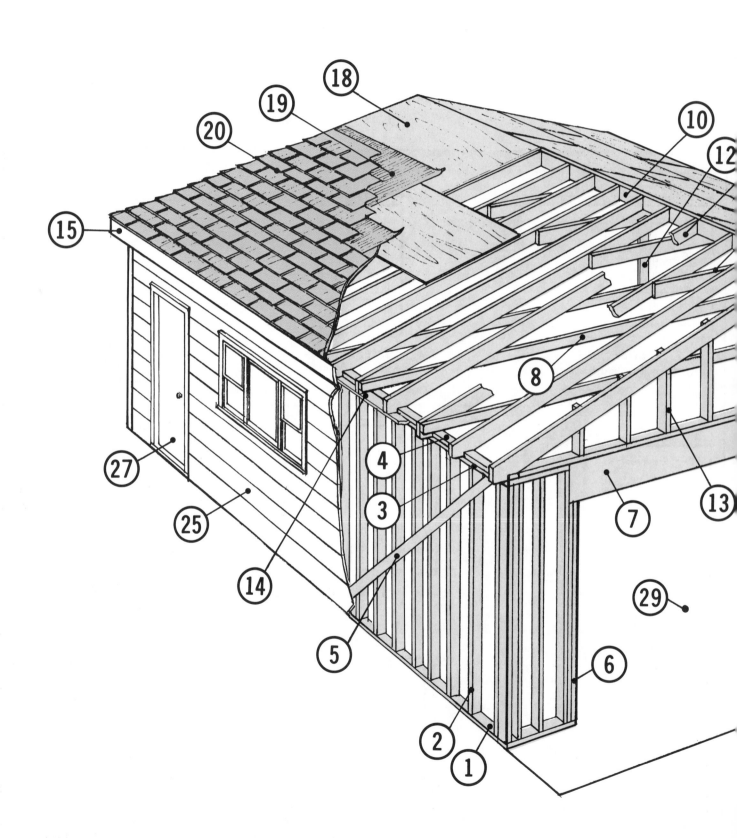

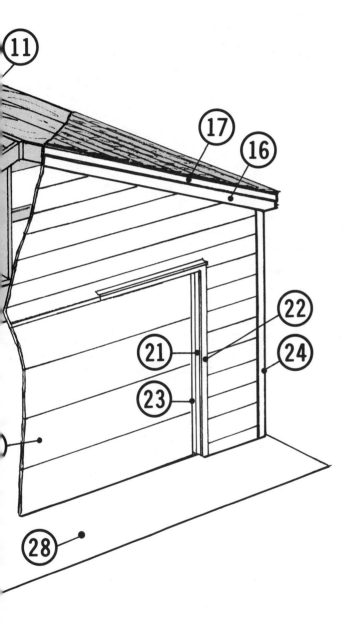

1. Treated Bottom Plate
2. Studs
3. Top Plate
4. Tie Plate
5. Corner Bracing
6. Cripple Studs
7. Garage Door Header
8. Rafter Ties
9. Rafters
10. Ridge Board
11. Collar Ties
12. Hangers
13. Gable Studs
14. Soffit
15. Fascia
16. Fascia (Rake)
17. Gable Shingle Mold
18. Roof Sheathing
19. Roofing Felt
20. Shingles
21. Doorjamb
22. Trim
23. Door Stop
24. Corner Boards
25. Siding
26. Sectional Garage Door
27. Service Door
28. Concrete Apron
29. Concrete Floor Slab

KNOW THE GENERAL PROCEDURE BEFORE YOU START

Before you can do a creditable job, you need to bone up on some of the basics of materials. The drawing at the bottom of this page and pages 26 and 27 are detailed views of the garage structure. They give you a good picture of the materials and techniques with which you will be working. A little time spent here will save you hours later.

Get a good helper. Some of the jobs require another set of hands, especially the foundation and framing stages.

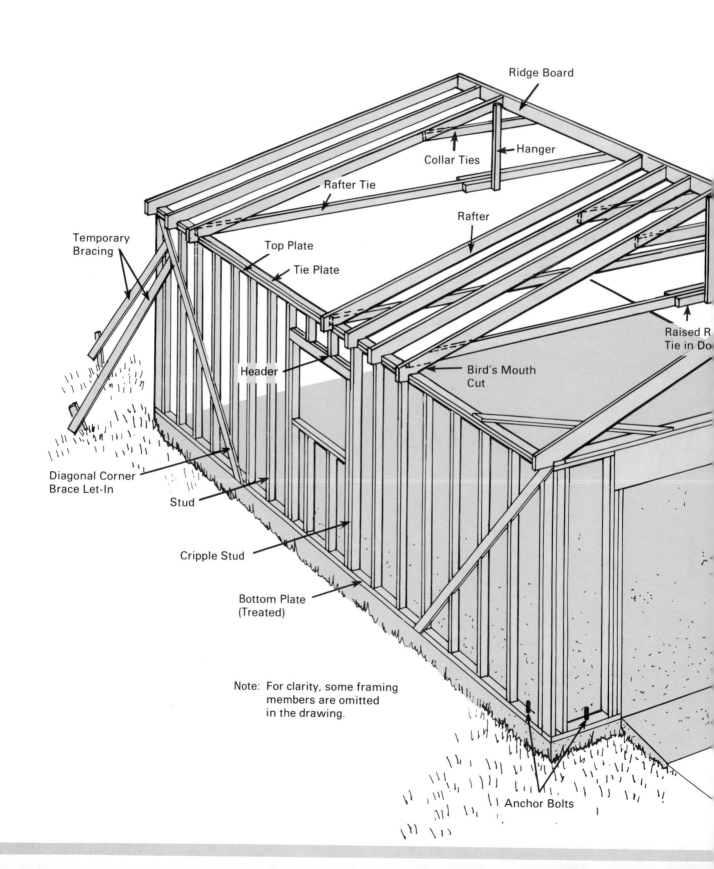

Ridge Board

Collar Ties

Hanger

Rafter Tie

Rafter

Temporary Bracing

Top Plate

Tie Plate

Raised R
Tie in Do

Header

Bird's Mouth
Cut

Diagonal Corner
Brace Let-In

Stud

Cripple Stud

Bottom Plate
(Treated)

Note: For clarity, some framing
members are omitted
in the drawing.

Anchor Bolts

NAILING SCHEDULE FOR STRUCTURAL MEMBERS		
Material	Number and type of nail	Spacing of nail
Plate to stud—end nail	2-16d	—
Stud to plate—toe nail	4-8d or 3-16d	—
Doubled studs—face nail	16d	24" o.c.
Doubled top plates—face nail	16d	16" o.c.
Rafter ties to plate—toe nail	2-16d	—
Rafter ties to parallel rafters—face nail	3-16d	—
Rafter tie to plate—toe nail	2-16d	—
1" brace to each stud and plate—face nail	2-8d	—
Roof rafters to ridge or hip rafters—toe nail	4-16d	—
face nail	3-16d	—
Collar ties to rafters—face nail	3-8d	—
1/2" plywood sheathing	6-6d at edges 12" at intermediate supports	
1/2" fiberboard sheathing	1-1/2" galvanized roofing nails 3" at edges 6" at intermediate supports	

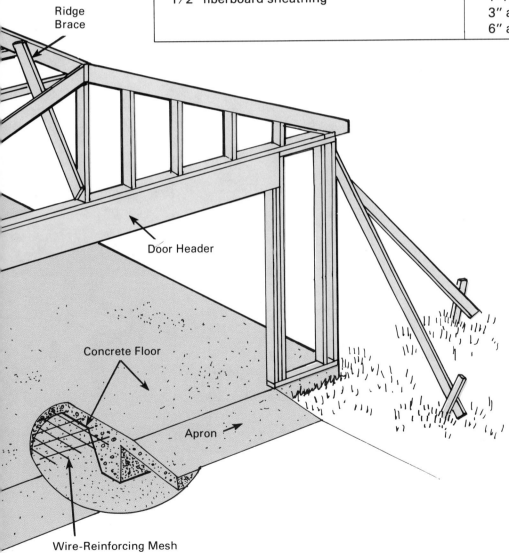

Ridge Brace

Door Header

Concrete Floor

Apron

Wire-Reinforcing Mesh

ESTABLISHING LOT BOUNDARIES BY THE LOT SURVEY

Before you can begin construction of the garage foundation, the precise boundaries of the building site must be verified by means of a lot survey conducted by a professional surveyor. Lots are normally recorded on maps kept on file by the local building or zoning authorities. By studying these maps and records, the lot surveyor will determine and stake out the precise boundaries of your property. By measuring from the proper reference points, the surveyor will establish the front two corners of the lot. These reference points can be the street curb, the center of the road bordering the lot, or special markers placed in the sidewalk. Once the front corners are marked out, a transit level is most often used to establish the two rear corners of the lot.

Once the lot boundaries are set, you can set up lines showing the exact location of the building, taking into account any setback guidelines set by local building codes. The information required to lay out the foundation can be found on the garage blueprints. It is also helpful to design a plot plan showing the location and dimensions of the planned garage, driveway, and sidewalks. (See pages 85 and 86 to lay out your plot plan.)

LAYOUT OF THE GARAGE SITE

Accurately locating the four corners of the building will in turn establish boundaries for the foundation. The site is layed out using batter board set back from the corners of the planned building in an L-shaped arrangement. Setting them back from the actual building site allows you to maintain an accurate reference point as you dig footings and construct the foundation.

Batter boards are made of pointed stakes connected with 4' lengths of 1 × 4 lumber. Each batter board should form an accurate right angle when checked with a framing square. Batter board tops must be level with each other all the way around. Check for this with a mason's line level. To set up batter boards:

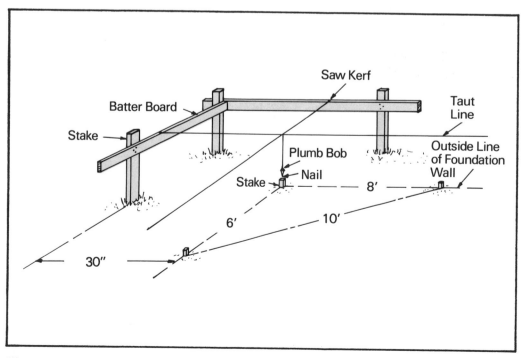

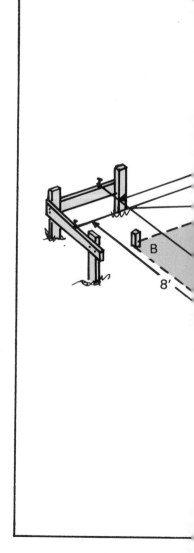

1. Accurately locate one corner of the building and drive stake A at that point.
2. Measure out along the long side of the building to the next corner. Drive in stake B at this point. Drive a small nail into the stakes and connect with tightly drawn twine.
3. Measure out the approximate positions of corners C and D and drive stakes at these points. Use a framing square to form an approximate right angle at these corners. Run twine from stakes B to C, C to D, and D to A.
4. You will now erect batter boards and adjust stake locations to form a true square or rectangular layout. Erect batter boards so that each corner stake is lined up directly on the diagonal from the opposite corner as illustrated. Use the line level to check that all batter boards are level with each other.
5. Stretch mason's twine between the batter boards so it is aligned directly over stakes A and B. When perfectly aligned make a saw kerf in the batter boards to make a permanent reference point and tack the twine fast.
6. Stretch twine over stakes B and C. It must form a perfect right angle with twine A-B. Check for a right angle using the 6/8/10 method. Measure 6' out along twine A-B and 8' along twine B-C. Mark these points with pins. The diagonal between these two pins should measure 10'. Adjust the position of twine B-C until it does and then notch the batter board at stake C and fasten off line B-C.
7. Using the 6/8/10 method lay out twine C-D and D-A. At each corner carefully measure from the point where the twine lines cross each other to set building dimensions. Drop a plumb line at this intersecting point and set stakes in exact positions.
8. Check the final layout by measuring the diagonals on the layout. They must be equal in length. If they are not, recheck your measurement and make proper adjustments.

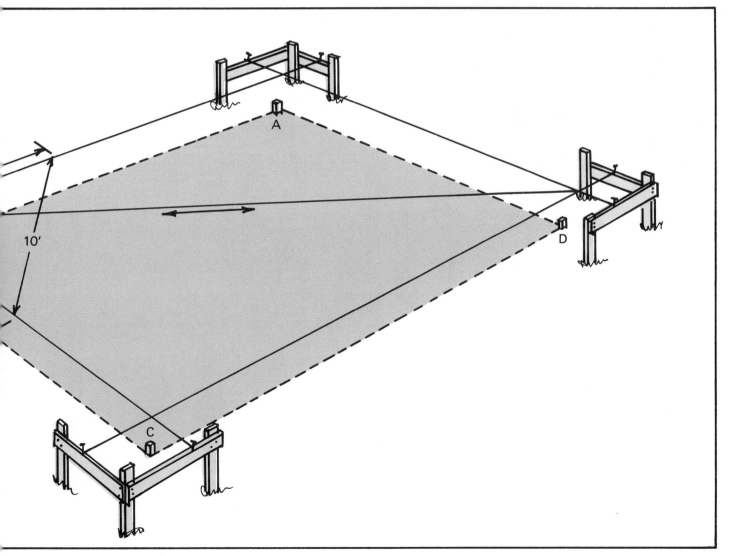

PREPARING YOUR GARAGE FOUNDATION

INVERTED T-SHAPED FORMS

The type of foundation you use will depend on your local climate and local building codes. In warmer climates you might only need a simple slab foundation such as those discussed on pages 18 and 19. In colder areas, where the foundation must reach below the frost line, several different designs can be used. The most common is the inverted T-foundation shown below. Whichever type you require, be certain to build a substantial and level foundation. It can save you plenty of problems later in the construction sequence, such as when you frame and level walls.

Placing concrete footings and foundations is hard work and can be tricky for the unexperienced. So this is one stage in the construction you might want to rely on professionals or friends with experience in working with concrete. Forms must be strongly constructed of sturdy lumber. To keep a large job manageable, divide the areas up into convenient sections that you and your crew can pour and finish in one day's time.

The spread footing of an inverted T-foundation provides good bearing on all soil types. Low T-foundations often have the footing and wall poured at the same time. These monolithic pourings eliminate the cold joint between footer and wall and prevent moisture seepage at this joint.

For high T-foundations, the footer and walls are poured separately. Immediately after the concrete footer has been placed, pieces of 2 × 4 lumber, called key strips, are often pressed into the concrete. Centered on the footing, these strips form keyways in the footing as it hardens. These keyway grooves help secure the foundation wall to the footing.

As you can see from the illustrations below, several different methods can be used to tie the bottom or sole plate of the wall framing to the foundation wall. Special ties can be embedded in the wet concrete once it begins to set, but the most common method is anchor bolts.

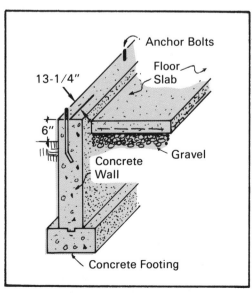

Special T-Lock Anchors

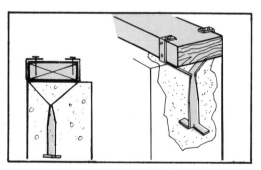

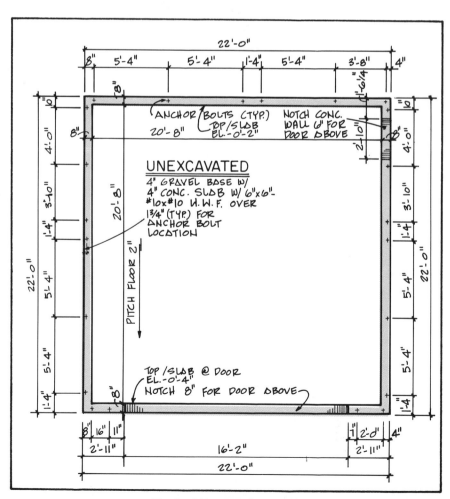

HOW TO POUR A CONCRETE FOOTING

FORMS FOR FOOTINGS

Typical footings are twice the width of the wall they tie into, but local building codes can vary from this rule of thumb. When the soil is firm and uniform, use an earth form for the footing by simply digging a trench to the required width and depth. When the soil is too soft to hold its form, wood forms for footings and foundation walls will be needed. Several designs are illustrated on this page. Concrete is very dense, so build and reinforce the forms strongly. Remember, if you plan to constuct a masonry wall on the footing, its top surface must be as level as possible. See page 20 for estimating materials and concrete amounts.

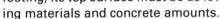

1. Lay out the footings using twine and batter boards as a guide for the trench. Use twine as a guide for your forms once the trench is dug.

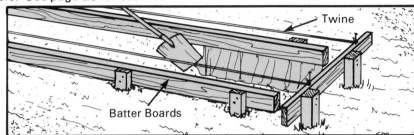

1

2. Level the bottom of the trench and tamp it firm. On sloping ground, use a stepped trench. The trench bottom must be below the frost line.

2

3. Build the forms using the batter boards as a guide for positioning. Support reinforcing steel using brick or stone. Suspend the keyway strip from cleats as shown.

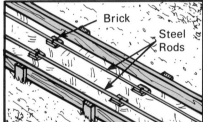
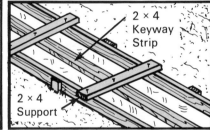

3

4. Coat the forms lightly with release agent or oil. Pour the concrete into the forms, working out air pockets with a flat shovel. Work the concrete into all corners and along edges of the form.

5. Level the concrete with the top of the form using a straight length of short lumber as a screed. Work back and forth in a short sawing motion. Knock down high spots and fill all voids. Remove the keyway strip as soon as the concrete will hold its shape.

4

6. Cure the concrete for four days. Cover it with burlap or plastic sheeting to retain moisture, and lightly spray the concrete with water once or twice daily to keep the surface wet during curing.

FORMWORK FOR FOUNDATION WALLS

Once you understand the principles of formwork for concrete walls, you should be able to handle the formwork for your garage's foundation wall. Most importantly, the form must be strong to withstand the pressure of the wet concrete and the rough treatment it will receive during the pour.

Foundation wall forms are constructed of plywood sheathing, 2 × 4 lumber framing and studs, wooden spacers, and wire ties. Sheathing forms the mold. The frame and studs support the sheathing. Spacers maintain wall thickness, support the form, and resist pressure exerted by the concrete. Ties hold the form sides together.

BUILDING FORMS

Build long forms in sections. The individual sections should be slightly taller than the planned finished foundation wall and no more than 8' in length.

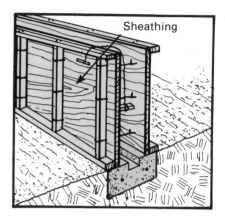

With the lumber laying flat on the ground, construct a frame of 2 × 4s on edge. Next, nail 2 × 4 studding into this frame, spacing studs on 16" centers, closer if the wall is particularly thick and will be poured all at one time.

The studded frame is now ready for the sheathing, either 1/2" or 5/8" thick plywood. Lay the sections down, sheathing sides face to face so you can drill holes for the wire ties. Drill 1/8" holes for the wire ties adjacent to the studs as shown. Plan on using plenty of ties to hold the forms together.

Spacers and ties are used to assemble the sections and maintain the proper spacing between them. Spacers are made of 1 × 2 or 2 × 4 lumber cut to the same length as the finished wall thickness. Plan to put in spacers every 2' both vertically and horizontally. Wire ties should be made of heavy gauge (8 or 9 gauge) iron wire. Cut the ties long enough to encircle opposing studs on either side of the forms, plus enough excess to comfortably twist the ends together.

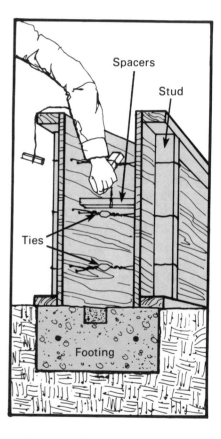

Tilt the two sections upright, face to face, and spaced at the wall thickness. Tack the sections together with several crosspieces to make working easier. Thread the 8 to 9 gauge wire ties through the form and around the studs, twisting the wire ends together. Place a 1 × 2 or 2 × 4 spacer near the tie.

Place a stick between the wires inside the form and twist the wire tight as illustrated. Do this for all spacers and ties. Tie pull wires on all spacers you will not be able to reach when the pour begins. You must remove all spacers as the pour proceeds.

Place the assembled form in position on the footer. Assemble additional sections, butting sections together and nailing through adjacent framing members to create the finished continuous wall form. The running length of the forms should be slightly longer than the planned wall length so that you can cleat in stop boards at the end of the forms.

A properly constructed form is self-supporting, but it must be plumbed and tied in place with braces so it will stay in position during the pour. Nail the bottom of the form to stakes driven firmly in the ground. This will prevent lifting. Prevent lateral movement by installing 2 × 4 angle braces.

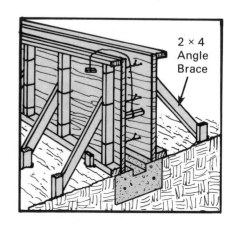

Prior to making the pour, coat the forms with concrete release agent or oil to make it easier to remove the form. See page 20 for the tools you'll need to place the concrete, plus tips on estimating the amount of concrete needed.

CASTING A CONCRETE WALL

Once the foundation footing has been placed and properly cured, you can set the wall forms in place, align, plumb, and secure them, and then make the wall pour. The steps involved in this process include: mounting the forms, pouring and tamping the concrete, striking, floating, and troweling the top edge smooth to accept the bottom plate, and installing the anchor bolts or special anchor ties.

1. Mount the forms on the cured footing, centering them over the keyway. See page 14 for more details on securing the forms in place.

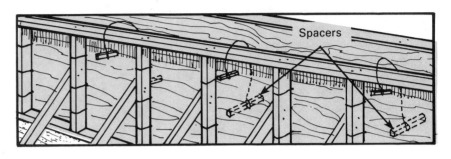

2. Pour the concrete into the forms, working in 6- to 8-inch layers. Do not stop the work once you begin, or "cold joints" between layers will result and cause cracks in the foundation wall. Work the concrete well up against the sides of the form. Tamping the side of the forms with a hammer will help settle the concrete and avoid air pockets. Pull out the spacers as you proceed.

3. Strike the concrete level with the top of the form using a board as a screed as you did with the footing. For a smoother surface, work the top surface with a wooden or steel trowel.

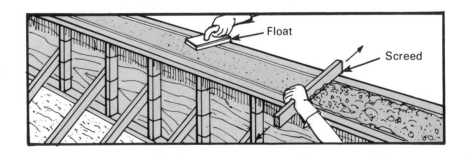

4. If you are going to use anchor bolts to secure the framing sill to the foundation, insert the anchor bolts at the proper spacing as soon as the concrete is firm enough to support them. Cure the concrete for four days as you did the footing. Remove the forms after curing.

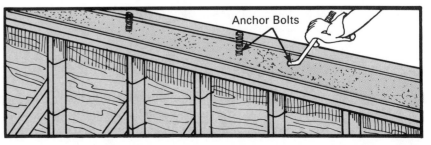

BUILDING CONCRETE BLOCK FOUNDATION WALLS

Concrete block can also be used to construct the foundation wall on the footing. The running bond shown in these illustrations is most commonly used. It allows the block cores to line up, making steel reinforcing and grouting easy.

Use the same type of mortar that is used in bricklaying, but mix it a little on the stiff side to make buttering the block a little easier. The mortar will also be less likely to squeeze out of the joints. Also do not wet the block before beginning work as you would with brick.

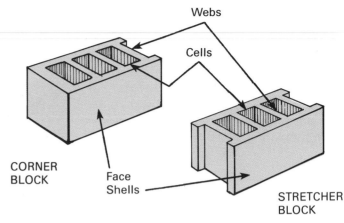

CORNER BLOCK

Webs

Cells

Face Shells

STRETCHER BLOCK

1. Start the lead in a corner, laying a bed of mortar 2" thick for three or four block. Lay the corner block carefully and press it down to an accurate 3/8" thick mortar joint. Butter the ends of the next blocks and place each 3/8" from the previous block. Use a level to align, level, and plumb the lead.

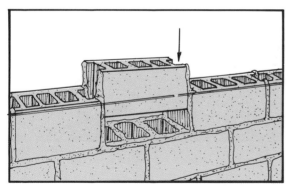

3. Begin leads at each corner and work to the middle. Lay blocks between the leads. To fit the closure block, spread mortar on all edges of the opening and butter the ends of the closure block. Set it carefully in place and check alignment, levelness, and plumbness.

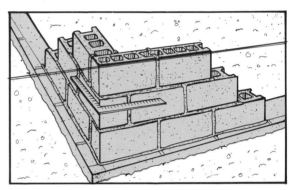

2. Continue laying block to complete the lead. Check for squareness at the corner. Use a mason's line to maintain a straight line as you work. All mortar joints are 3/8".

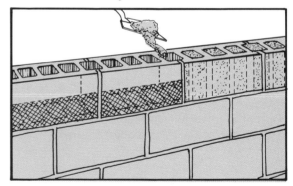

4. To cap the wall, cover the cores of the next-to-last course with metal screening before laying the top course. Fill the cores in the top course with mortar.

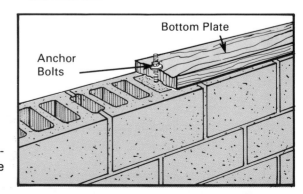

Bottom Plate

Anchor Bolts

5. You can now sink anchor bolts into the mortar-filled top course. This will tie down the sill plate on which the garage framing will rest.

POURING THE CONCRETE FLOOR FOR A T-SHAPED FOUNDATION

Placing a concrete floor inside a T-foundation is similar to placing a slab foundation as described on pages 18 and 19. Rather than using forms, the foundation walls are the outside boundaries of the floor. Be sure the area inside the foundation boundaries is properly backfilled, leveled, and prepared with a gravel base and reinforcing mesh set on stones to raise it slightly off the gravel.

Placing a large slab is hard work so be sure you have two or three helpers, one or two wheelbarrows and shovels, plus all the concrete finishing tools you'll need (see page 20).

The height of the foundation walls makes screeding over the entire length of the slab impossible, so stake a number of temporary screeding guides inside the foundation. These will help you level the concrete to the correct thickness, usually 4". Once the initial screeding is complete, the guides are pulled out and these voids filled with concrete. You can also use a wide wooden darby to level the concrete.

As the work progresses, watch the concrete carefully. In hot or windy weather, the first sections might be setting up too fast, while you are still pouring the remaining sections. If this is the case, some members of your crew will have to begin finishing work a little sooner than planned. Never add water to the concrete to keep it workable until you are ready to finish the concrete.

After each section has been screeded, use a wooden bull float or darby to smooth it. Once initial smoothing has been completed, wait for the concrete to lose its initial shine before beginning final troweling. For a smooth finish use a wooden float. A really slick finish requires a steel trowel. For large slabs, use a rented power trowel.

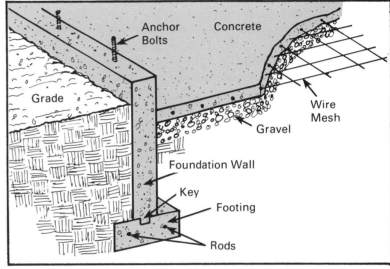

Anatomy of T-shaped Foundation With Concrete Slab Floor

Bull floating levels ridges and fills voids left after striking. It is used for large areas.

FOUNDATION DETAILS FOR TURNED-DOWN MONOLITHIC SLABS

If you live in an area where frost upheaval is not a problem, a basic slab foundation can be used for your garage. Again, check the local building requirement in your area, and follow their specifications. Here's a checklist of common code requirements:

1. Slab thickness of 4″ with the top of the slab set 6″ above the surrounding soil.
2. A footing ditch dug around the perimeter of the slab—6″ wide at the base of the trench and 12″ deep or deeper, depending on frost considerations. Footing must contain a layer of reinforcing steel rod 3″ up from the base of the footing trench.
3. You'll need a gravel base under the slab 3″ to 4″ thick. A layer of 6″-square welded wire must be placed in the slab. Raise this wire 2″ off the gravel using stones, brick halves, or broken concrete to support it.
4. Anchor bolts embedded in the footing to accept the mudsill for framing the garage. Use 10″ long anchors embedded 7″ deep in concrete on 6′ centers not more than 12″ away from the end of a mudsill. Do not place anchors in doorways.

SLAB FORMS

Level the site. Small depressions can be filled with gravel and concrete. Use 2 × 8 lumber for the forms and brace it securely. Begin laying out the forms at the highest point of the site and work to the lowest. The top of the forms should be perfectly level. In some cases, you might prefer a slope of 1/2″ in 20′ toward the overhead garage door location to help with drainage. Double-check dimensions and squareness by measuring the diagonals across the forms. Once forms are square and level, install bracing stakes every 3′ or so on the outside face of the forms. Be sure to use sufficient bracing driven

well in firm ground. The inside dimensions of the forms will be the finished outside dimension of the slab, exclusive of any apron.

This apron can be poured as part of the slab or added later. If it is part of the slab, bevel apron form boards so the apron slopes to a point level or slightly above the driveway surface.

Once the forms are in place, dig the required footing trench at the inside form perimeters and place the required reinforcing steel in the trench. Lay the gravel base and wire mesh according to code requirements, and wet the gravel before the pour. (See page 20 for tools needed and estimating concrete needs.)

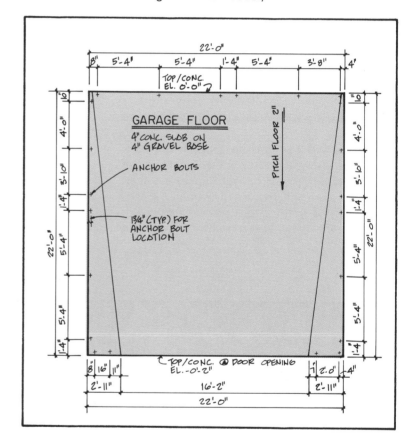

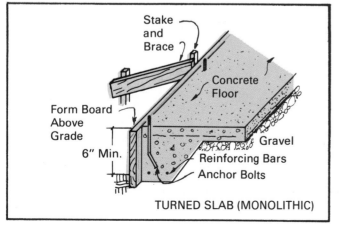

TURNED SLAB (MONOLITHIC)

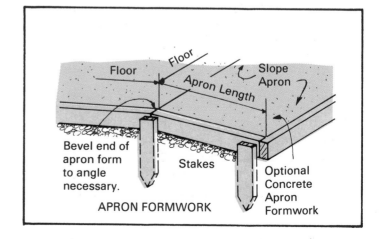

APRON FORMWORK

POURING THE CONCRETE SLAB

Have the local building inspector check the forms prior to the pour date. If electrical service is desired, place the electrical conduit in proper location prior to the pour.

PLACING

Have adequate help, wheelbarrows, and tools ready when the concrete truck arrives. Start by pouring in the area farthest away from the truck, using wheelbarrows to move the concrete. Begin by filling the footing trench. For larger areas, break the work into smaller sections by installing temporary screeding guides. When one section is poured move to the next section while helpers screed off the first. Rap on the outside of the form boards to help settle the concrete. Be sure all voids are filled. Pay special attention along the perimeters of the form boards. Remove the temporary screed guides while filling in these voids.

FINISHING

Once the concrete has lost its initial shine, begin finishing it with a bull float. Larger floats have a handle like a broom. If you are using smaller hand floats, use toe and knee boards placed on the concrete so you can kneel on the concrete without leaving much of an impression. Move the float in long sweeping motions.

Anchor bolts should be placed after the concrete has been screeded and bull floated. Place the bolts 1-3/4" away from the edge of the slab. Double-check spacing of bolts and alignment.

For a coarser finish, bull floating is all that is required. For a slicker, smoother finish, use a steel trowel to go over the work once bull floating is complete. Use a light touch so you don't gouge the concrete surface. Before the concrete hardens completely, take a trowel and cut between the edge of the concrete and the form.

CURING

Once all finishing is completed, mist down the slab with water, and cover it with a layer of plastic, burlap, or straw. Keep the surface moist for four days as the concrete cures.

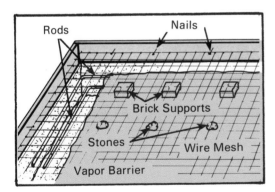

Steel reinforcing rods and wire mesh are laid into place over gravel and optional plastic vapor barrier.

Workers level concrete slab with a strike board.

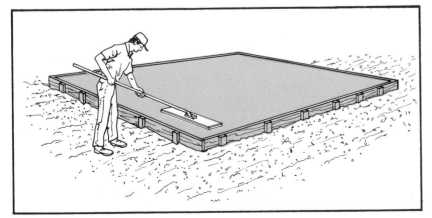

Smooth concrete surface with a bull float.

Add anchor bolts.

Some of the Tools Needed

Tamper

Wheelbarrow

Bull Float

Shovel

Broom

Edger

Steel Trowel

Groover

Kneeler and Pads

Mason's Trowel

Wood Float

Carpenter's Square

Mason's Level

Hand Darby

Hammer

Hand Sledge

Twine

Chalk Line

Tape Measure

Striker

Estimating Cubic Yards of Concrete for Slab*

Thick-ness, inches	Area in square feet (width × length)					
	10	25	50	100	200	300
4	0.12	0.31	0.62	1.23	2.47	3.70
5	0.15	0.39	0.77	1.54	3.09	4.63

To find the amount of concrete required for for a 4-in. thick driveway 20 ft. wide by 20 ft. long, for example, first figure the number of square feet: Multiplying 20 ft. by 20 ft. gives 400 sq. ft. From table

300 sq. ft. = 3.70 cu. yd.
100 sq. ft. = 1.23 cu. yd.
Total: 400 sq. ft. = 4.93 cu. yd.

With a perfect subgrade and no losses from spillage, 5 cu. yd. might be enough. But for insurance against contingencies, the order should be increased to 5-1/2 cu. yd. It is always better to have some concrete left over than to run short.

*Does not allow for losses due to uneven subgrade, spillage, etc. Add 5 to 10 percent for such contingencies. Does not allow for turn- down areas.

Calculating Concrete Volume

Concrete is measured in cubic yards. To calculate cubic yards, multiple thickness (in inches) × width (in feet) × length (in feet) and divide by 12. This gives cubic feet. Divide this number by 27 to determine cubic yards. Take measurements carefully. While you do not want to order more than your needs, being short can cause major problems.

CHOOSING LUMBER FOR FRAMING

Nearly all types of general construction is done using softwoods, such as Douglas fir or southern pine. As a rule softwoods are less expensive, easier to work with, and more readily available than hardwoods, which are normally reserved for fine finishing work.

LUMBER SIZES

In general, construction softwood lengths run from 6' to 20' in 2' increments. *Dimension lumber,* graded primarily for strength, is used in structural framing. These pieces range from 2" to 4" thick and are at least 2" wide. *Beams and stringers* are structural lumber 5" thick or more, having a width at least 2" greater than the thickness. *Posts and timbers* are heavy construction members 5" × 5" or larger with a width not exceeding thickness by more than 2".

The actual final dimensions of lumber are slightly smaller than the nominal dimensions. The chart below lists nominal and actual width and thickness for common structural lumber.

Draw up a materials list from your plans, listing the number, size, and length of the pieces you'll need. Prices will be by the linear foot or by the board foot for larger orders. Linear feet considers only the length of the piece, for example, twenty 2 × 4s, 10' long or 200 linear feet of 2 × 4. However, board feet pricing considers total volume, for example, a 2 × 4 that is 10' long would be (2 × 4 × 10) ÷ 12 = 6.66 or 6-2/3 board feet.

Select lumber that is seasoned or dried. Green lumber can cause problems as it shrinks. Dimension lumber is usually stamped MC-15 (15% moisture content) or S-DRY (19% moisture content or less).

When you can, select vertical grain lumber as shown below, and be on the lookout for the common lumber defects illustrated. They are not considered in grading.

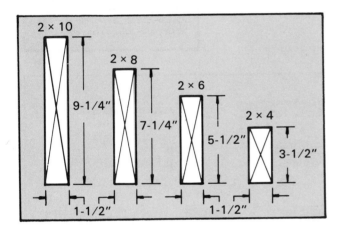

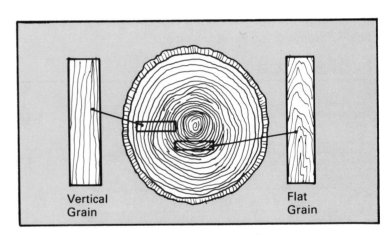

Vertical Grain

Flat Grain

STANDARD DIMENSIONS OF SURFACED LUMBER	
Nominal size	Surfaced (actual) size
1 × 2	3/4" × 1-1/2"
1 × 3	3/4" × 2-1/2"
1 × 4	3/4" × 3-1/2"
1 × 6	3/4" × 5-1/2"
1 × 8	3/4" × 7-1/4"
1 × 10	3/4" × 9-1/4"
1 × 12	3/4" × 11-1/4"
2 × 3	1-1/2" × 2-1/2"
2 × 4	1-1/2" × 3-1/2"
2 × 6	1-1/2" × 5-1/2"
2 × 8	1-1/2" × 7-1/4"
2 × 10	1-1/2" × 9-1/4"
2 × 12	1-1/2" × 11-1/4"
4 × 4	3-1/2" × 3-1/2"
4 × 10	3-1/2" × 9-1/4"
6 × 8	5-1/2" × 7-1/2"

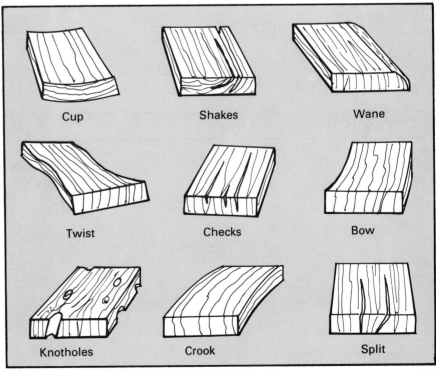

Cup   Shakes   Wane

Twist   Checks   Bow

Knotholes   Crook   Split

NAILS AND FASTENERS FOR FRAMING AND FINISHING

Nails are the most common fastener used in framing and construction. Nail lengths are indicated by the term penny, noted by a small letter d. In most cases, nails increase in diameter as they increase in length. Most framing for heavier construction is done with common nails. The extra thick shank of common nails has greater strength than most other types. A wide thick head spreads the load and resists pull-through. The larger head also makes a good target for a hammer.

Box nails are similar in shape and use to common nails, but they have a slimmer shank that is less likely to split wood. Finishing nails are used in work where you do not want the nail head to show such as in trim and fascia work. Casing nails, similar to finishing nails but with a thicker shank and angular head, are used for heavier work such as adding casings around windows and doors.

Spiraled shanks rotate slightly for better holding power as you drive the nail in wood. Annular-ring nails also provide extra holding power, especially in softer woods.

Discuss your project with your local hardware or building supply dealer to determine the best nail and fastener selections for the work.

Screws create neat, strong joints for finished work, such as door and window treatments. Heavy-duty lag screws are also used in some types of heavier framing and construction.

FINISHING NAIL SELECTION CHART

SIZE	LENGTH	GAUGE	APP. # PER LB.
10d	3"	11½	120
8d	2½"	12½	190
6d	2"	13	310
4d	1½"	15	600
3d	1¼"	15½	870
2d	1"	16	1000

TABLE OF COMMON NAILS

SIZE	LENGTH	GAUGE	#PER LB.
2d	1"	15	840
3d	1¼"	14	540
4d	1½"	12½	290
5d	1¾"	12½	250
6d	1"	11½	160
7d	2¼"	11½	150
8d	2½"	10¼	100
9d	2¾"	10¼	90
10d	3"	9	65
12d	3¼"	9	60
16d	3½"	8	45
20d	4"	6	30
30d	4½"	5	20
40d	5"	4	16
50d	5½"	3	12
60d	6"	2	10

This table of common nails shows the approximate number of nails you get in a pound. You'll need more pounds of larger sizes to do a job. For outside jobs, get galvanized or cadmium-plated nails. Aluminum nails are a bit expensive unless you're doing a small project.

Nail Selection Chart

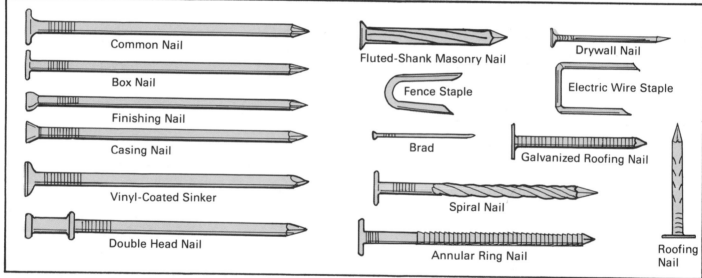

Common Nail
Box Nail
Finishing Nail
Casing Nail
Vinyl-Coated Sinker
Double Head Nail
Fluted-Shank Masonry Nail
Fence Staple
Brad
Spiral Nail
Annular Ring Nail
Drywall Nail
Electric Wire Staple
Galvanized Roofing Nail
Roofing Nail

Screw Selection Chart

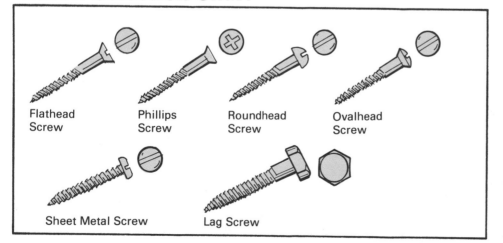

Flathead Screw
Phillips Screw
Roundhead Screw
Ovalhead Screw
Sheet Metal Screw
Lag Screw

SCREW SELECTION CHART

Size	Length	Size	Length
0	1/4-3/8	9	1/2-3
1	1/4-1/2	10	1/2-31/2
2	1/4-3/4	11	5/8-31/2
3	1/4-1	12	5/8-4
4	1/4-11/2	14	3/4-5
5	3/8-11/2	16	1-5
6	3/8-21/2	18	11/4-5
7	3/8-21/2	20	11/2-5
8	3/8-3	24	3-5

This chart shows sizes and the lengths in which they're available. The larger sizes come in longer lengths. Most jobs call for sizes 6 to 12 in ½ to 3 inch lengths. Check size and length before you buy.

SELECTING YOUR DOOR

Exterior doors are commonly 1-3/4" thick, not less than 80" high, and 32" to 36" wide. Exterior doors should be solid-core or solid-panel construction. This means the space between the front and back surfaces is filled with either wood or partical board. A solid door offers more security and is less subject to warping that can be caused by humidity and differences in temperature between inside and outdoors.

A well-made solid-panel door uses vertical-grain wood carefully fitted together with glue and dowels. The door consists of the vertical stiles, horizontal rails, and the solid filler material. The door can be flush or have panel insets. Flush doors are made by covering the stiles and rails with thin sheets of veneer plywood.

Decide on the number and sizes of doors before framing begins. Be sure all framing openings for doors (and windows) are correctly dimensioned and squared. The door manufacturer provides dimensioning information, so be sure to obtain this data from your building supply dealer.

Door Styles

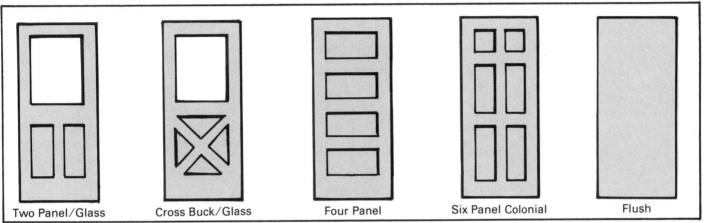

Two Panel/Glass Cross Buck/Glass Four Panel Six Panel Colonial Flush

SELECTING YOUR WINDOWS

Most garage designs incorporate one or more windows to admit light and provide a view to the outdoors. Fixed window designs do not open but provide excellent protection against air infiltration. Openable windows include awning, double hung, casement, slider, and single unit designs as shown. Casement windows usually open outward and provide excellent ventilation. Single- and double-hung windows, as their names imply, have one or two sashes that open. They provide slightly less ventilation when compared to casement designs. Awning windows are hinged at the top or bottom and open either in or out. They provide excellent airflow and are easy to clean from the exterior.

Selection is more or less a matter of personal taste, but there might be some local code restrictions. Know the exact frame-out dimensions for the windows you select before beginning work.

Window Styles

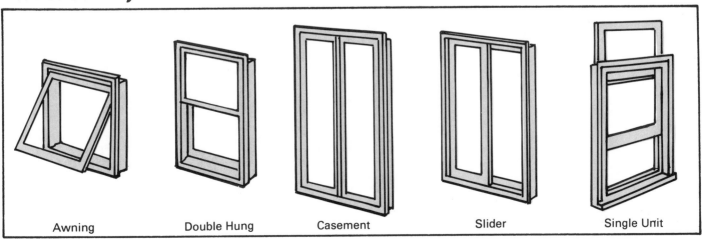

Awning Double Hung Casement Slider Single Unit

Typical Garage Floor Plan (Wall Panel System)

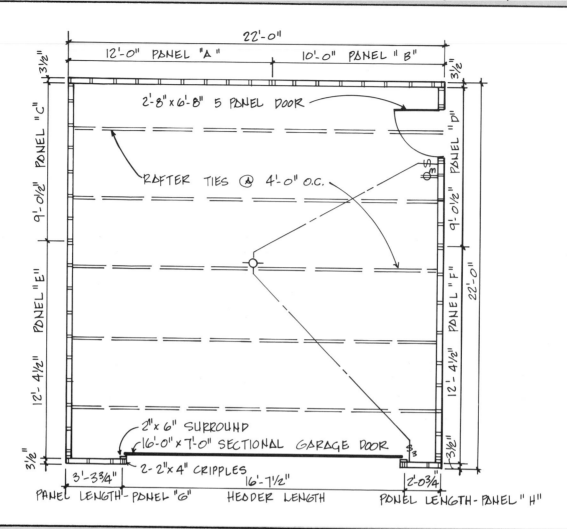

22'-0"

12'-0" PANEL "A"   10'-0" PANEL "B"

3½"

2'-8" x 6'-8" 5 PANEL DOOR

RAFTER TIES @ 4'-0" O.C.

PANEL "C"   9'-0½"

PANEL "D"   9'-0½"

PANEL "E"   12'-4½"

22'-0"

PANEL "F"   12'-4½"

3½"

2" x 6" SURROUND
16'-0" x 7'-0" SECTIONAL GARAGE DOOR

3½"   3½"

3'-3¾"   2- 2" x 4" CRIPPLES   2'-0¾"
PANEL LENGTH - PANEL "G"   16'-7½"   PANEL LENGTH - PANEL "H"
                            HEADER LENGTH

Typical Garage Wall and Roof Framing Plan

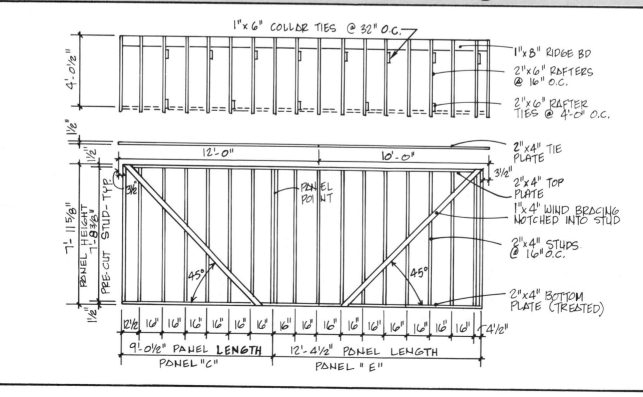

1" x 6" COLLAR TIES @ 32" O.C.

4'-0½"

1" x 8" RIDGE BD

2" x 6" RAFTERS @ 16" O.C.

2" x 6" RAFTER TIES @ 4'-0" O.C.

1½"
1½"
1½"

12'-0"   10'-0"

2" x 4" TIE PLATE

3½"

PANEL POINT

2" x 4" TOP PLATE

1" x 4" WIND BRACING NOTCHED INTO STUD

2" x 4" STUDS @ 16" O.C.

45°   45°

7'-11⅝" PANEL HEIGHT 1-8⅜" PRE-CUT STUD-TYP.

3½"

2" x 4" BOTTOM PLATE (TREATED)

1½"

12½" 16" 16" 16" 16" 16" 16" 16" 16" 16" 16" 16" 16" 16" 16" 4½"

9'-0½" PANEL LENGTH   12'-4½" PANEL LENGTH
PANEL "C"   PANEL "E"

GARAGE WALL FRAMING

The basic wall framing outlined on the following pages can be used for whatever roof system you choose. If you are not working from a professionally drawn plan, it is a good idea to layout your plan on graph paper before your begin. Use the plan to determine the materials you will need and to make any special alterations to the basic framing, such as opening for doors and windows. You should also determine if the siding you plan to install will require three studs at the corners for nailing and if sheathing is necessary.

Wall framing includes a bottom or sole plate, evenly spaced wall studs, and a top plate. A tie plate is added to the top plate once the walls are raised. Extra studding and headers are needed at door and window openings.

In most cases, walls are built of 2 × 4 studs and plates with studs spaced on 16" centers. Two by six lumber can also be used with a stud spacing of 24". Bottom plates should be treated lumber to resist rot.

SET BOTTOM PLATE

The bottom plate rests on the foundation walls, flush with the outside edge of each wall. Snap chalk lines to set the plate's inner edge and check for squareness by measuring the diagonals. Position the bottom plates against the anchor bolts and mark off the hole locations. When using standard 1/2" diameter anchor bolts, drill 3/4" holes at these locations. Temporarily install bottom plates over the anchor bolts to check positioning.

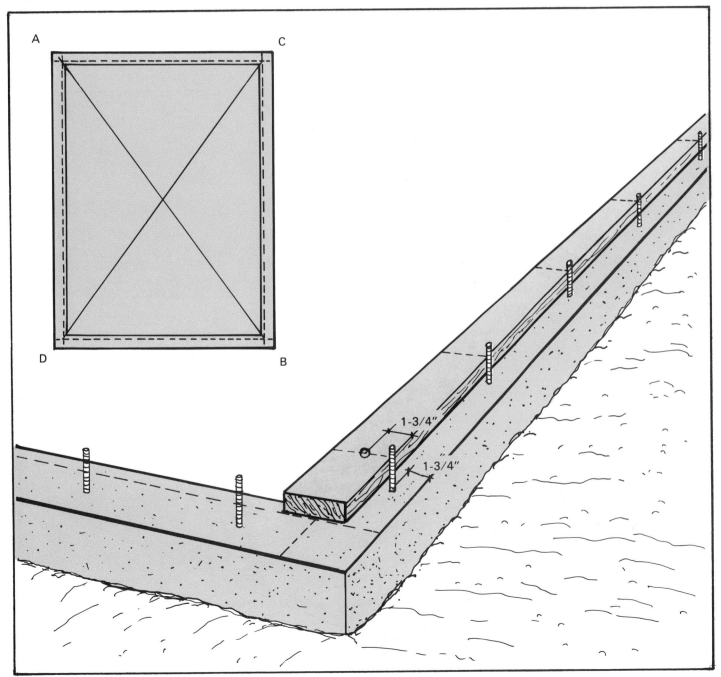

CONSTRUCTING THE BASIC WALL FRAME

To begin, cut both the top and bottom plates to length. In most cases, you will need more than one piece of lumber for each plate. So locate the joints at stud centers and offset joints between top and bottom plates by at least 4'.

Lay the top plate against the bottom plate on the slab as illustrated below. Beginning at one end, measure in 15-1/4" and draw a line across both plates. Measure out farther along the plates an additional distance of 1-1/2" from this line, and draw a second line. The first interior stud will be placed between these lines.

From these lines, advance 16" at a time, drawing new lines, until you reach the far end of the plates. Each set of lines will outline the placement of a stud, with all studs evenly spaced at 16" on center. If you are using studs on 24" centers, the first measurement in from the edge would be 23-1/4".

ASSEMBLING THE PIECES

Unless you are using precut studs, the next step is to measure and cut the wall studs to exact length. Position the plates apart on the slab and turn them on edge with stud marking toward the center. Place the studs between the lines and nail them through each plate with two 16d common nails.

FRAMING CORNERS

Where walls meet, you might need extra studs to handle the corner tie to the adjacent wall. These extra studs should be added to the ends of the longer two of the four walls. The exact positioning of these extra corner studs is shown at the bottom on page 29.

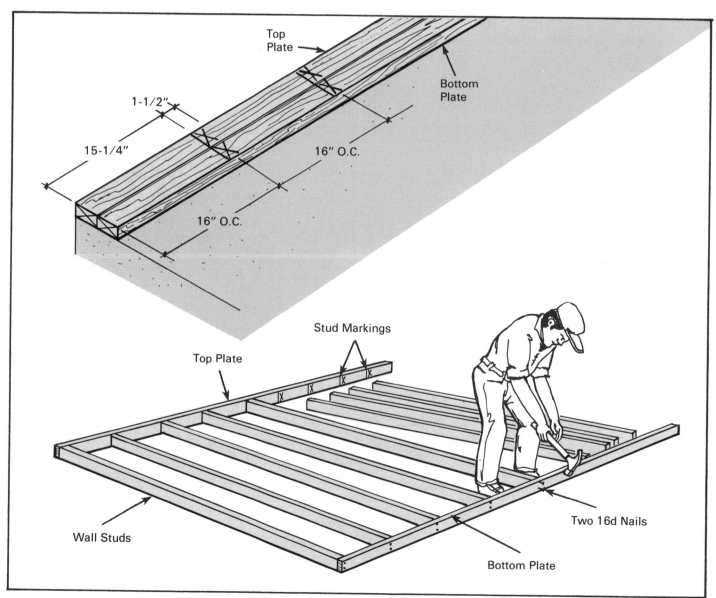

Top Plate

Bottom Plate

1-1/2"

15-1/4"

16" O.C.

16" O.C.

Stud Markings

Top Plate

Wall Studs

Two 16d Nails

Bottom Plate

DOOR AND WINDOW FRAMING

At door and window openings there is no stud support, so a header constructed of two lengths of 2 × 4 with a 1/2" piece of plywood sandwiched between them is needed. The plywood makes the header the same width as the studs. Headers are always installed on edge as shown. The spaces above door openings and above and below windows are framed with cripple studs spaced 16" on center. Study the illustrations to become familiar with the king stud and trimmer stud locations used in framing doors and windows.

The rough framed door should be 1 1/2" higher than the usual 80" actual door height and 2 1/2" wider than the door to account for doorjamb material. When the 1 1/2" bottom plate is cut from the opening, this adds the needed 1 1/2" in extra height.

In addition to cripple studs, king studs, and trimmer studs, window framing also uses a rough sill to support the window. Headers should be set at the same height as door headers. The rough frame should be 1/4" to 1/2" larger on all sides to accept the window. (See page 46).

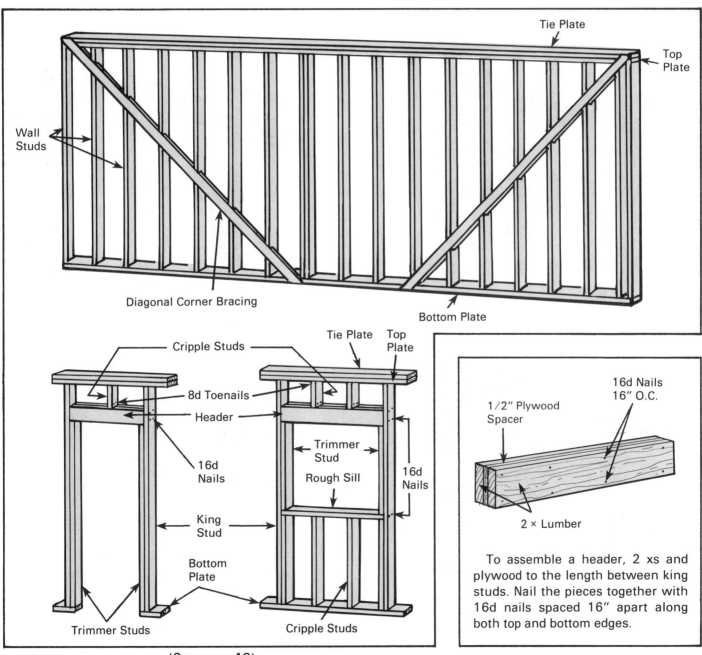

To assemble a header, 2 xs and plywood to the length between king studs. Nail the pieces together with 16d nails spaced 16" apart along both top and bottom edges.

(See page 46)

DIAGONAL BRACING

Structures with plywood siding normally do not require bracing, but all others do. The two most commonly used types of bracing are wooden "let-in" bracing made of 1 × 4 stock and metal strap bracing.

LET-IN BRACING

This type of wooden bracing runs from the top outside corners of the wall to the bottom center of the wall. It forms a V-shaped configuration as shown on page 27. These braces are set into notched studs and are prepared while the wall frame is still lying on the slab.

Lay the 1 × 4 on the frame with one end at a top corner and the other end as far out on the bottom plate as possible without running into any door or window opening. Mark the underside of the brace where it overhangs the top and bottom plates to determine the angle at which the plates cross. Also mark both sides of the studs and plates at each point the brace crosses them. Notch the studs at these locations by making repeated cuts with your circular saw. Use a hammer and wood chisel to knock out any stubborn chips. Trim the ends of the 1 × 4 and put the brace in place. Hold it in place with a single nail until the wall is raised and plumbed. Then nail the brace fast with 8d nails wherever it crosses a plate or stud.

METAL STRAP BRACING

Commonly available in 10' to 12' lengths, this type of bracing is nailed to the outside of the studded walls after they are raised, square, and plumb. Metal bracing is thin enough not to obstruct the exterior wall sheathing.

The straps have predrilled holes every 2" sized to accept an 8d nail. Strap bracing must always be installed in crossed pairs, similar to a large X design.

STEP 1   Mark bracing locations.

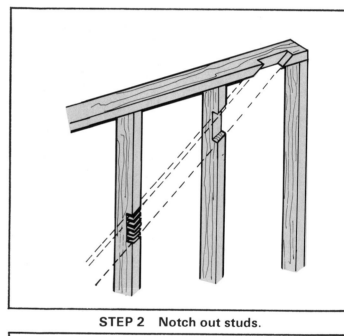

STEP 2   Notch out studs.

STEP 3   Nail bracing into stud locations.

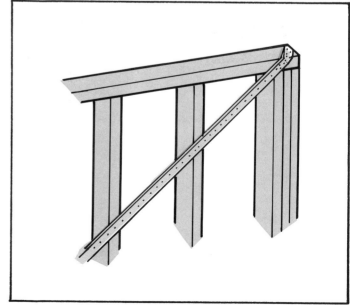

Alternate Metal Strap

RAISING THE WALLS

Most walls can be raised by hand if enough help is available on the job site. It is advisable to have one person for every 10' of wall for the lifting operation. See page 30.

The order in which walls are framed and raised can vary from job to job, but in general, the longer exterior walls are raised first. The shorter exterior walls are then raised and the corners are nailed together.

Once the first wall is framed out, there are only a few short steps until it is up and standing. Slide the wall along the slab until the bottom plate lies near the anchor bolt at the floor's edge. To raise the wall have your workers grip it at the top plate in unison and work their hands beneath the plate. Now everyone walks

down the wall until it is in the upright position. As you tilt the wall up, slip the bottom plate in place over the anchor bolts.

To brace the wall, tack 2 × 4 braces to the wall studs, one at each end and one in the middle if the wall is particularly long. Tie these braces into stakes driven firmly in the ground. Now secure the wall to the anchor bolts using washers and nuts.

To check alignment, use a carpenter's level to check the wall for plumb along both end studs on adjacent faces. If the wall is out of plumb, loosen that brace, align the wall, and secure the brace again. If an end stud is warped, bridge the warp with a straight board. When both ends are plumb, adjust the middle.

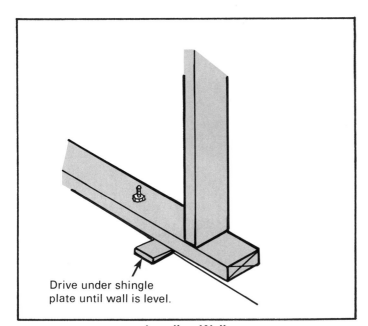

Drive under shingle plate until wall is level.

Leveling Wall

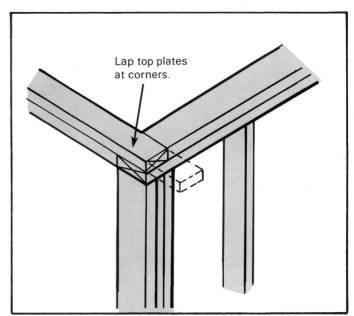

Lap top plates at corners.

Corner Detail Top Plates

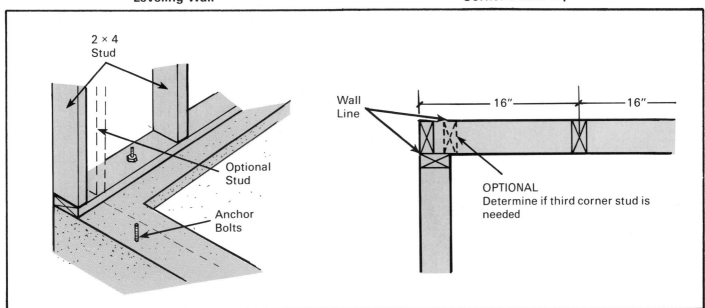

2 × 4 Stud

Optional Stud

Anchor Bolts

Wall Line

16"   16"

OPTIONAL Determine if third corner stud is needed

Corner Detail

LEVELING AND CORNER DETAILS

Once raised, the wall should also be checked for levelness. If needed, it can be shimmed level using tapered cedar shingles driven between the foundation and the bottom plate. Once the wall is plumb and level, tighten the anchoring nut to their final tightness.

At corners, nail through the end walls into the stud using 16d nails staggered every 12". When the walls are up, you can then add the 2 x 4 tie plates to the top plates on each wall. These tie plates lap over onto adjacent walls as shown in the illustrations on pages 29 and 30.

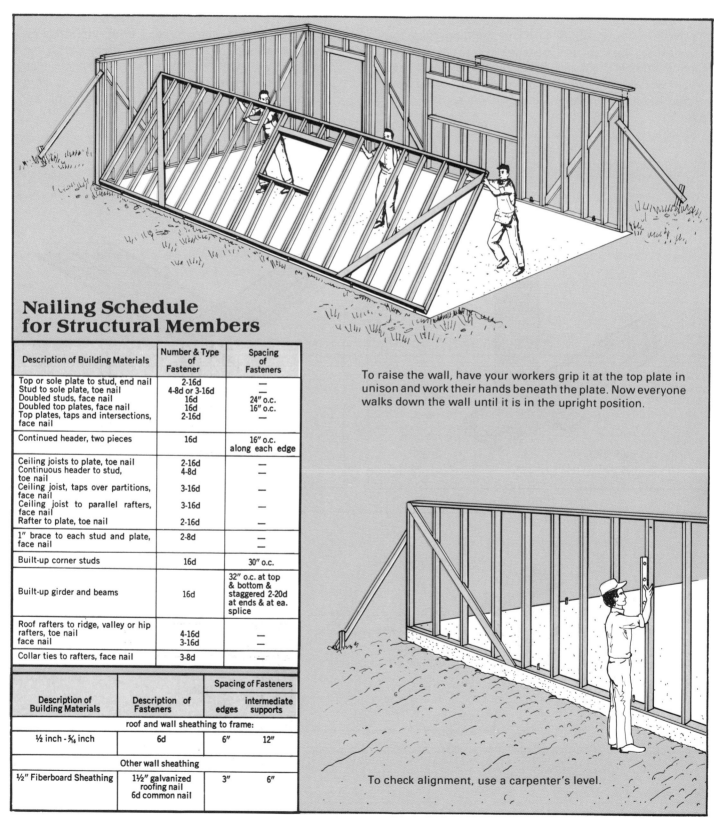

Nailing Schedule for Structural Members

Description of Building Materials	Number & Type of Fastener	Spacing of Fasteners
Top or sole plate to stud, end nail	2-16d	—
Stud to sole plate, toe nail	4-8d or 3-16d	—
Doubled studs, face nail	16d	24" o.c.
Doubled top plates, face nail	16d	16" o.c.
Top plates, taps and intersections, face nail	2-16d	—
Continued header, two pieces	16d	16" o.c. along each edge
Ceiling joists to plate, toe nail	2-16d	—
Continuous header to stud, toe nail	4-8d	—
Ceiling joist, taps over partitions, face nail	3-16d	—
Ceiling joist to parallel rafters, face nail	3-16d	—
Rafter to plate, toe nail	2-16d	—
1" brace to each stud and plate, face nail	2-8d	—
Built-up corner studs	16d	30" o.c.
Built-up girder and beams	16d	32" o.c. at top & bottom & staggered 2-20d at ends & at ea. splice
Roof rafters to ridge, valley or hip rafters, toe nail	4-16d	—
face nail	3-16d	—
Collar ties to rafters, face nail	3-8d	—

Description of Building Materials	Description of Fasteners	Spacing of Fasteners	
		edges	intermediate supports
roof and wall sheathing to frame:			
½ inch - ⅝ inch	6d	6"	12"
Other wall sheathing			
½" Fiberboard Sheathing	1½" galvanized roofing nail 6d common nail	3"	6"

To raise the wall, have your workers grip it at the top plate in unison and work their hands beneath the plate. Now everyone walks down the wall until it is in the upright position.

To check alignment, use a carpenter's level.

FRAMING WITH METAL FASTENERS

When undertaking a large-scale construction project, such as your garage, you may find it easier to use a variety of metal fasteners and supports to tie beams together, hang joists, support posts, or brace walls. These metal fasteners come in different sizes to accommodate all sizes of structural lumber, and most hardware stores carry a large selection. In some areas, use of metal fasteners is optional, but in other regions where hurricanes and high wind factors are a problem, special connectors may be required by the building code.

JOIST HANGERS

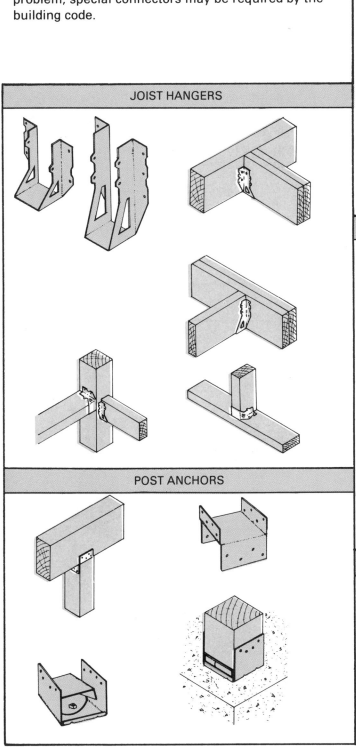

POST ANCHORS

FRAMING ANCHORS

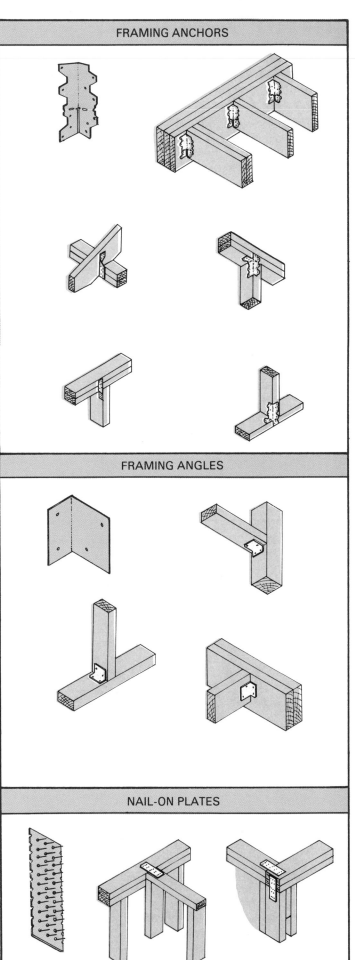

FRAMING ANGLES

NAIL-ON PLATES

ROOF FRAMING

Most roof designs are variations of the gable roof, in which evenly spaced pairs of *common* rafters tie the top plates and central ridge board together. Rafters are 2 × 4s, 2 × 6s, or 2 × 8s, depending on span, spacing, load and roof slope, and are installed on 16-inch or 24-inch centers. Check with your local building office for help with these variables. At the peak, rafter boards butt against a central ridge board. The ridge board can be either 1 × or 2 × lumber and is one size wider than the rafter lumber. For example, use 6-inch wide wood if the rafters are 2 × 4s, 8-inch wood with 2 × 6s, and so on. Slope, or pitch, is referred to in terms of *unit rise* in *unit run. Unit run* is fixed at 12 inches. *Unit rise* is the slope over those 12 inches. A rise of 4" over 12" is a slope of "4 in 12."

CUTTING THE RAFTERS

A *common* rafter has three cuts: the *plumb* cut to form the angle where the rafter meets the ridge board, the *bird's mouth* notch to fit the top plate, and the *tail* at the end of the overhang. Professionally prepared plans often have a template or diagram for a master or "pattern" rafter. Cut two rafters off the master and check them for accuracy before cutting the others. Use a steel carpenter's square to mark the cuts.

RAISING THE ROOF

With ridge board and rafters cut, you can raise the roof. You'll need three people. Nail an upright 2 × 4 for each of the end rafters flush against the middle of the end top plate. One person then lines up one end rafter with the end of the side top plate and ties it in with three 16d nails. The second raises and holds it at the correct slope against one of the 2 × 4s, while the third tack nails the two together. Do the same with the opposite end rafter, then align the ridge board between the top of the rafters and tie it in with three 16d nails through each rafter. Use 8d nails if the ridge board is 1 × lumber. The ridge board must be level, and the rafter ends must be flush with the sides of the ridge board. Repeat the process at the opposite end for a single-piece ridge board; for a two-piece ridge board, tie the rafters to the last spacing mark at the opposite end.

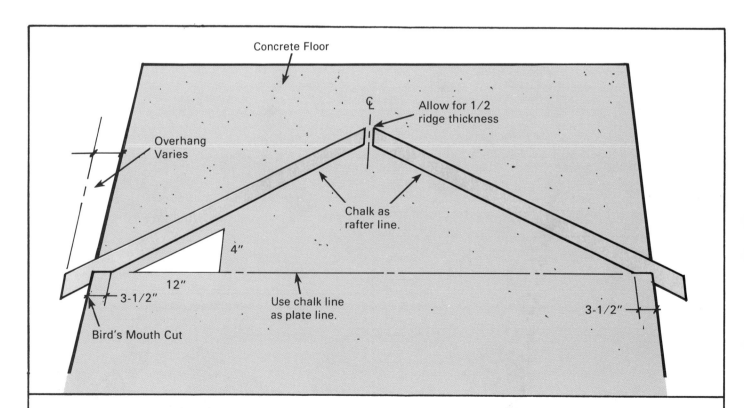

For those of us not familiar with a square, lay out the initial pair of rafters on the slab. Snap chalk lines to represent the bottom of the rafters and the plate line. Use the rise in 12" to establish the angle (for example, 4" in 12"). If they fit, use them as patterns for all other rafters.

LEVELING AND BRACING

Make sure the end rafters are plumb, and the ridge board is level and centered mid-span, then attach a diagonal brace between the ridge board and the 2 x 4 nailed to the top plate. Run the remaining rafters in pairs, attaching them to the ridge board first, then to the top plate. If a second ridge board is used, the process is repeated from the opposite end of the building. The junction of the ridge boards must be covered by two rafters. Use three 16d nails to tie rafters to rafter ties (joists) and cut ties to match the slope of the rafters.

Be sure to add collar ties and hangers before removing any shoring or bracing. Blocks can be needed on the eaves for extended overhangs.

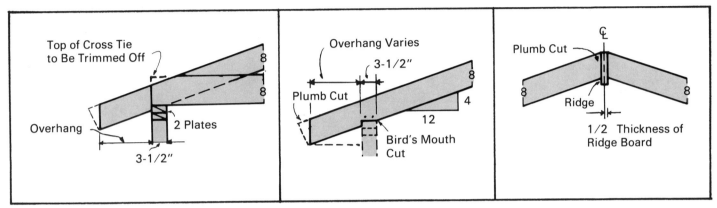

Rafter Cuts

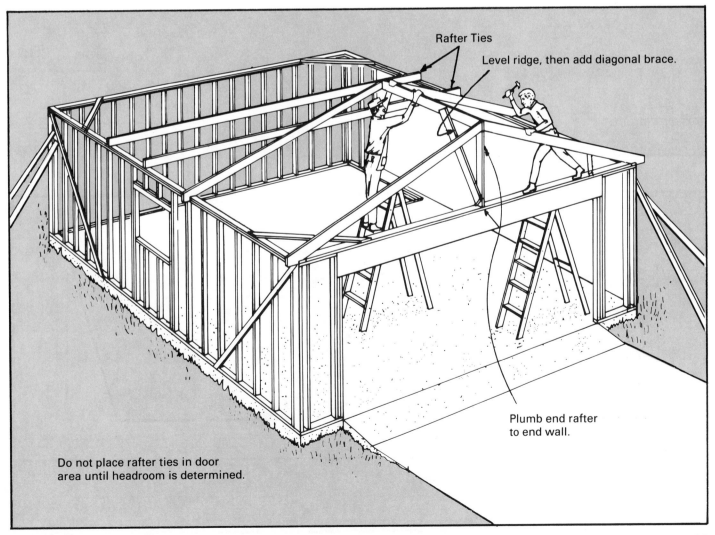

Rafter Framing

ROOF FRAMING CONTINUED

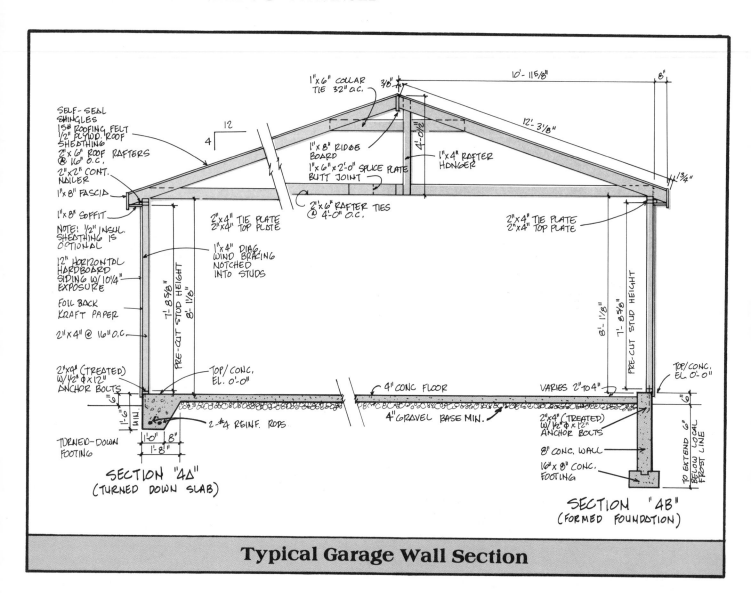

SELF-SEAL SHINGLES
15# ROOFING FELT
1/2" PLYWD. ROOF SHEATHING
2"x 6" ROOF RAFTERS @ 16" O.C.
2"x2" CONT. NAILER
1"x 8" FASCIA
1"x 8" SOFFIT
NOTE: 1/2" INSUL. SHEATHING IS OPTIONAL
12" HORIZONTAL HARDBOARD SIDING W/ 10 1/4" EXPOSURE
FOIL BACK KRAFT PAPER
2"x 4" @ 16"O.C.
2"x4" (TREATED) W/ 1/2" Ø X 12" ANCHOR BOLTS
TURNED-DOWN FOOTING

SECTION "4A"
(TURNED DOWN SLAB)

12
4

1"x 6" COLLAR TIE 32" O.C.
1"x 8" RIDGE BOARD
1"x 6"x 2'-0" SPLICE PLATE BUTT JOINT
2"x 6" RAFTER TIES @ 4'-0" O.C.
2"x 4" TIE PLATE
2"x 4" TOP PLATE
1"x 4" DIAG. WIND BRACING NOTCHED INTO STUDS

3'-0"
4'-0 1/2"
1"x 4" RAFTER HANGER
10'- 11 5/8"
8"
12'- 3 1/8"
1 3/4"

2"x 4" TIE PLATE
2"x 4" TOP PLATE

7'- 8 5/8" PRE-CUT STUD HEIGHT
8'- 1 1/8"

8'- 1 1/8"
7'- 8 5/8" PRE-CUT STUD HEIGHT

TOP/CONC. EL. 0'-0"
4" CONC. FLOOR
VARIES 2" to 4"
TOP/CONC. EL. 0'-0"
4" GRAVEL BASE MIN.
2"x4" (TREATED) W/ 1/2" Ø X 12" ANCHOR BOLTS
8" CONC. WALL
16"x 8" CONC. FOOTING
2- #4 REINF. RODS

6"
6"
1'-0"
1'-6" MIN.
1'-0" 8"
1'-8"
TO EXTEND 6" BELOW LOCAL FROST LINE

SECTION "4B"
(FORMED FOUNDATION)

Typical Garage Wall Section

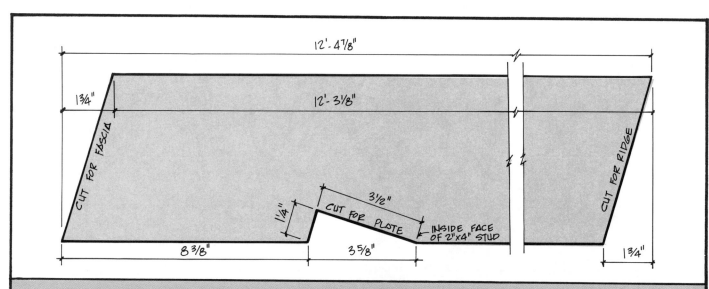

12'- 4 7/8"
12'- 3 1/8"
1 3/4"
CUT FOR FASCIA
CUT FOR RIDGE
1/4"
3 1/2"
CUT FOR PLATE
INSIDE FACE OF 2"x 4" STUD
8 3/8"
3 5/8"
1 3/4"

Typical Rafter Cutting Diagram

Blueprint plans are available for garages (see back of this book). Each garage plan includes rafter cutting templates to help you do the job easier.

ROOF FRAMING CONTINUED

As mentioned earlier, metal fasteners provide the strength nails alone can't provide. They also avoid the irritation of watching angled nails split the lumber you have so carefully cut and fitted.

Toenailing rafters to top and tie plates can be eliminated with the use of metal anchors and reinforcing angles. These plates provide solid support where the members cross. As you can see from the illustrations below, many different types of ties are available for roof framing work.

ROOF FRAMING CONTINUED

TRUSSED RAFTERS

Trussed rafters are often available from local lumber dealers. They are designed to span the full width of a structure from one exterior wall to the other. This leaves a large room free of supports. The use of preassembled trusses speeds the erection of the roof. Be certain to obtain your trusses from a reliable source who will custom design and build them to your needs.

ERECTING TRUSSES

It is advisable to have at least two other persons assisting you when erecting roof trusses. Have all walls securely braced. The steps to follow are:

1. With one person at each side wall of the structure and one at the center, place the trusses onto the top plate of the outside walls, upside down, Figure 36A.
2. Move the first gable end truss into position at the end of the building and swing it up into position with the man in the center working from the ground with a pole to push the center up, Figure 37A.

3. Center truss between side walls. Plumb truss and temporarily toenail in place. Brace gable truss down to ground stake to keep it plumb.
4. Repeat Step 3 at opposite gable end.
5. Place nails at peak of each gable truss. Run a string line from one end to the other and draw tight.
6. Tilt up one truss at a time. Be sure that the peak is exactly under string line. Space truss 24" apart measured from center to center. Laterally brace all trusses to keep them from tipping over. A 2 × 4 nailed to the top of each truss after it is plumb will help keep them in line until the roof sheathing is applied, Figure 37B.
7. Remove lateral bracing from the top of the trusses only after roof sheathing has been applied.
8. Fasten each truss to the top plate using metal framing anchors, use one at each end of the truss. (See page 35.)
9. Often construction blueprints call for a different size rafter than the top chord of a trussed rafter. If this is so, adjust the trim boards to accommodate the variance.

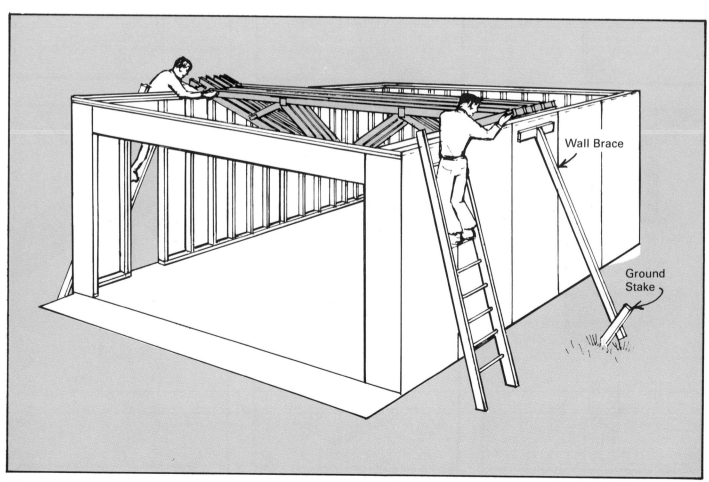

Wall Brace

Ground Stake

Figure 36A

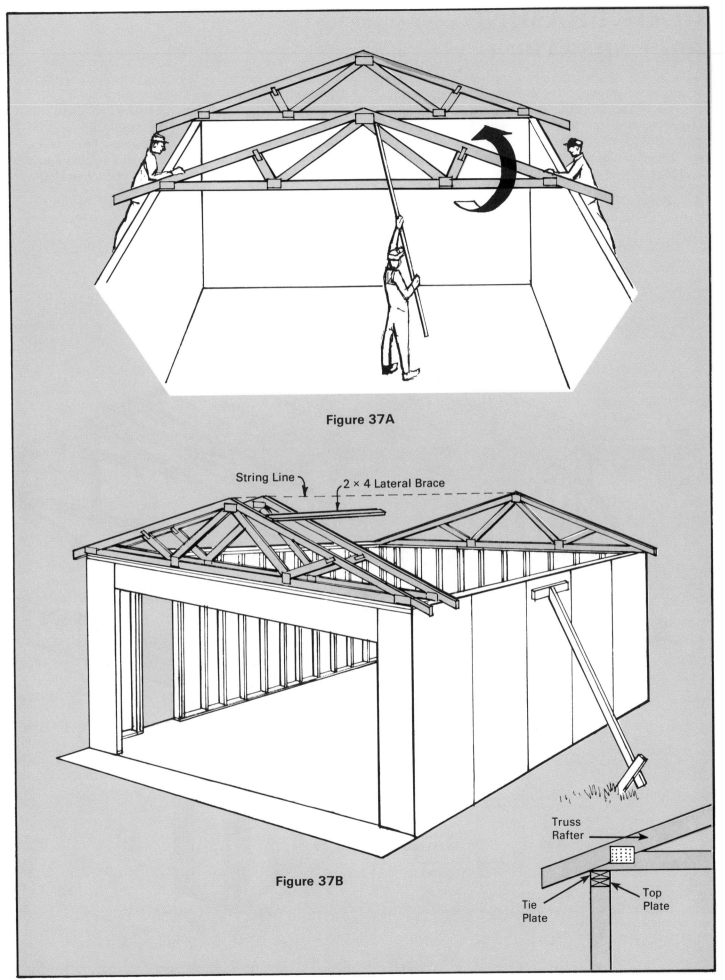

Figure 37A

String Line

2 × 4 Lateral Brace

Figure 37B

Truss
Rafter

Tie
Plate

Top
Plate

37

ROOF FRAMING CONTINUED
ROOF SHEATHING

Using 4' × 8' plywood panels covers large roof areas quickly, although 1 × 8s laid up tightly can also be used. The required thickness of the sheathing will vary with rafter spacing and local building code requirements, if any. Generally, the wider the rafters are spaced, the thicker the sheathing needs to be.

Stagger the sheathing, starting at the bottom, so that the end joints of adjacent sheets fall on different rafters. Space 6d nails 6" apart at sheet ends, and 12"

on center at intermediate rafters. If gable eaves have an overhang, extend the sheathing to cover it.

Note: Check garage door hardware and opener instructions before nailing rafter ties in place. Minimum clearance requirements between the top of the door opening and the bottom of the ties might require that the ties be set up off of the top plate. See Figure 38B.

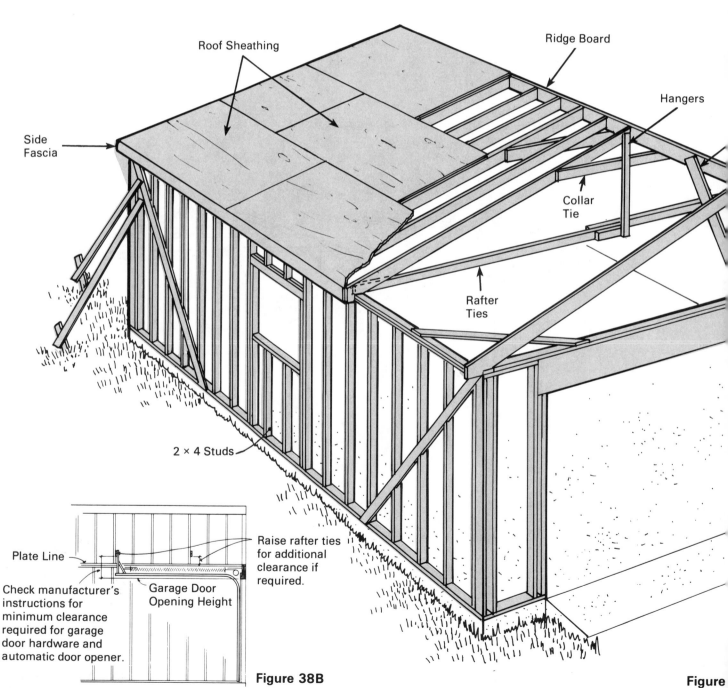

Roof Sheathing

Ridge Board

Hangers

Side Fascia

Collar Tie

Rafter Ties

2 × 4 Studs

Plate Line

Raise rafter ties for additional clearance if required.

Check manufacturer's instructions for minimum clearance required for garage door hardware and automatic door opener.

Garage Door Opening Height

Figure 38B

Figure

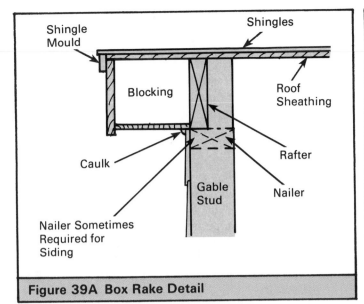

Shingle Mould

Shingles

Shingle Mould

Blocking

Roof Sheathing

Caulk

Rafter

Nailer

Gable Stud

Nailer Sometimes Required for Siding

Figure 39A Box Rake Detail

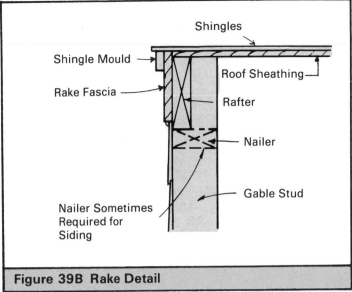

Shingles

Shingle Mould

Rake Fascia

Roof Sheathing

Rafter

Nailer

Gable Stud

Nailer Sometimes Required for Siding

Figure 39B Rake Detail

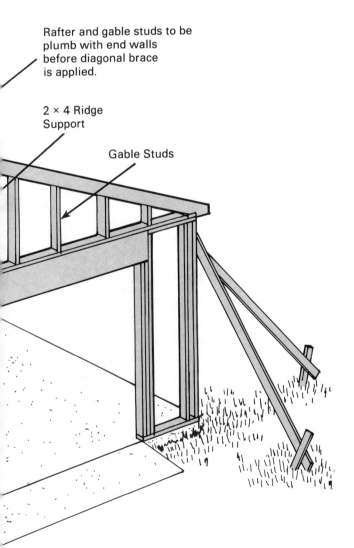

Rafter and gable studs to be plumb with end walls before diagonal brace is applied.

2 × 4 Ridge Support

Gable Studs

Note:
Before roof sheathing is in place, determine garage door hardware headroom and then add rafter ties to clear the hardware.

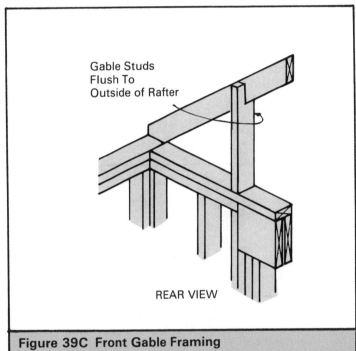

Gable Studs Flush To Outside of Rafter

REAR VIEW

Figure 39C Front Gable Framing

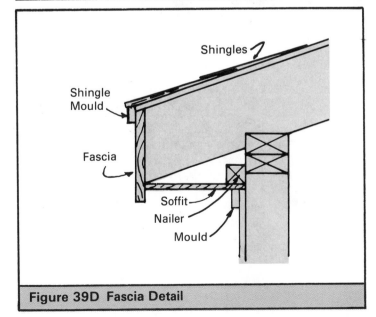

Shingles

Shingle Mould

Fascia

Soffit

Nailer

Mould

Figure 39D Fascia Detail

HIP ROOF FRAMING

Rafter lengths require some paperwork on hip roofs. Lay out a plan view of the roof on graph paper as shown in Figure 41B. The larger the scale, the greater the accuracy, so use a minimum 1" to 1' scale.

CALCULATING RAFTER LENGTHS

To determine rafter lengths, draw horizontal line A—B (Figure 41C). Locate A' by projecting up the scale height of the roof slope. A line between A' and B will give the angle for plumb and tail cuts on common and jack rafters, as well as common rafter length (except for the additional length at top for cutting angle). Lay hip roof out similarly: horizontal line A—C, and A'—C for hip length, allow enough length for angle cut.

For jack rafter lengths, lay out points X, Y, Z, and so on, along A—B and project up to A'—B. In addition to the plumb, tail, and bird's mouth cuts, jack rafters must also be cut to 45° across the narrow width (Figure 41A) to line up with the hip rafter.

ERECTING A HIP ROOF

To erect the hip roof, begin with the common rafters along the ridge (Figure 40A), or erect four common rafters if the building is square. Nail up rafter ties as well (Figure 41D). Before nailing the rafter ties in position, it is strongly suggested that you check for proper clearance for any planned garage door and garage door opener. Most garage doors require a minimum clearance between the top of the garage door opening and the bottom of the rafter ties. The door and opener manufacturer provides these clearances and you can check them with your building supplier. To gain the clearance required, it might be necessary to set the rafter ties up off the top and tie plate. See Figure 38B.

Nail hip rafters to corners, and use a temporary brace to create a slight crown in them (Figure 41D). Next, nail up jack rafters in opposing pairs connected to rafter ties. Use just one nail in each until all are in place, then adjust them to straighten the hip rafter and nail them in permanently.

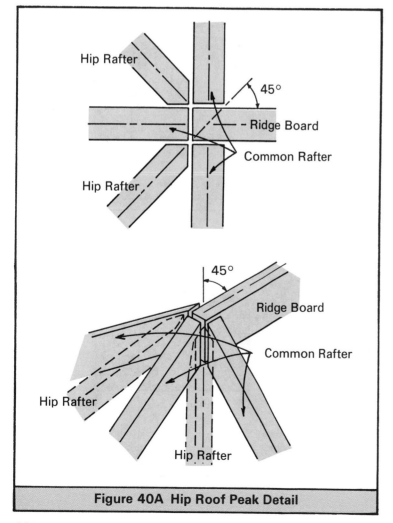

Figure 40A Hip Roof Peak Detail

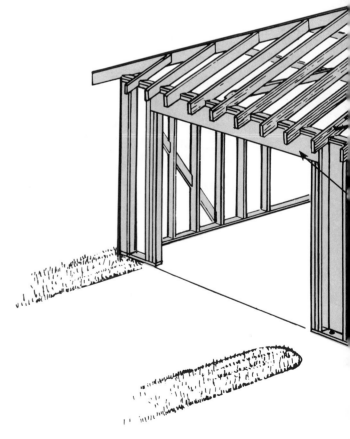

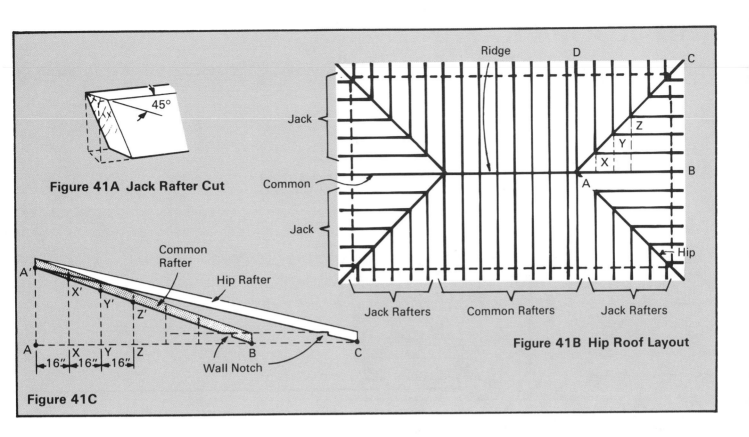

45°

Figure 41A Jack Rafter Cut

Ridge   D   C

Jack

Common

Jack

Z

Y

X

A

B

Hip

Jack Rafters   Common Rafters   Jack Rafters

Figure 41B Hip Roof Layout

Common Rafter

Hip Rafter

A'

X'

Y'

Z'

A   X   Y   Z   B   C

16"   16"   16"

Wall Notch

Figure 41C

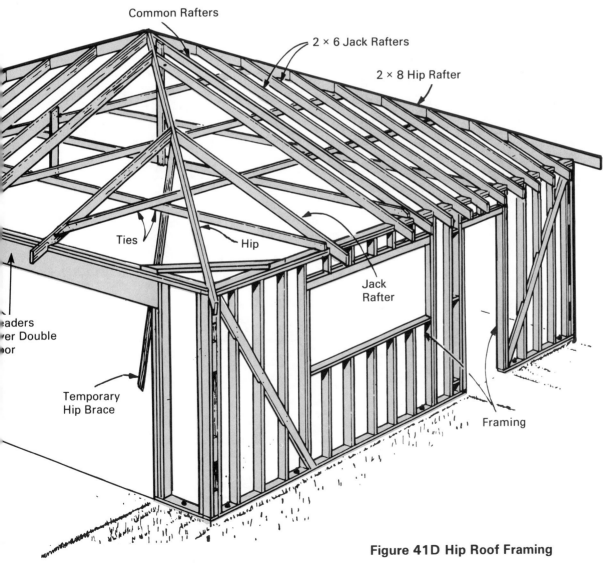

Common Rafters

2 × 6 Jack Rafters

2 × 8 Hip Rafter

Ties

Hip

Jack Rafter

aders
er Double
or

Temporary
Hip Brace

Framing

Figure 41D Hip Roof Framing

HIP ROOF FRAMING CONTINUED

Blueprint plans are available for hip roof garages (see back of this book). To help you do the job easier, each garage plan includes hip roof details and rafter cutting templates like this one below and also on the next page.

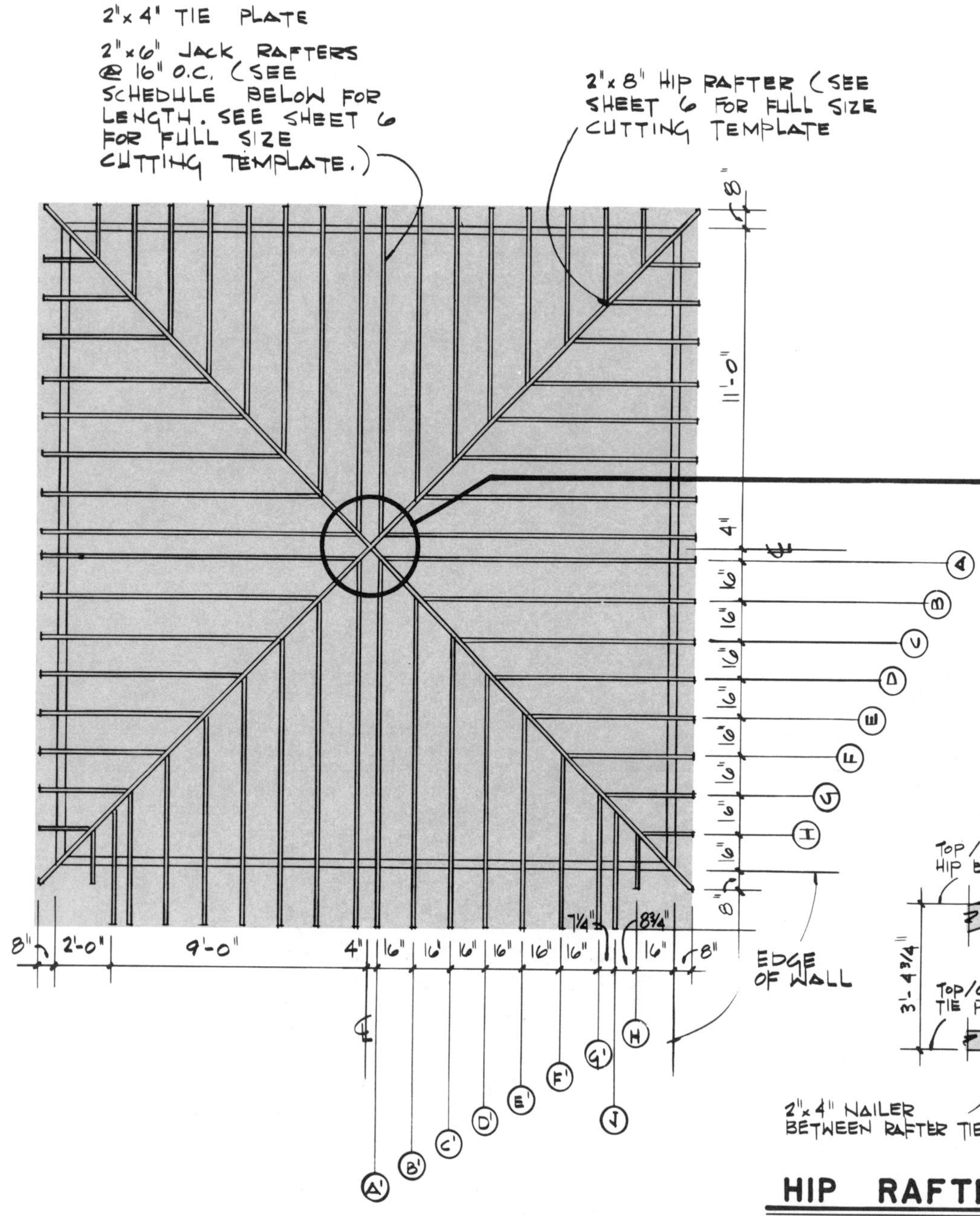

2"x 4" TIE PLATE
2"x6" JACK RAFTERS @ 16" O.C. (SEE SCHEDULE BELOW FOR LENGTH. SEE SHEET 6 FOR FULL SIZE CUTTING TEMPLATE.)
2"x 8" HIP RAFTER (SEE SHEET 6 FOR FULL SIZE CUTTING TEMPLATE
8"
11'-0"
4'
16"
8"
2'-0"
9'-0"
7 1/4"
8 3/4"
EDGE OF WALL
A
B
C
D
E
F
G
H
A'
B'
C'
D'
E'
F'
G'
J

RAFTER FRAMING PLAN

SCALE 1/4" = 1'-0"

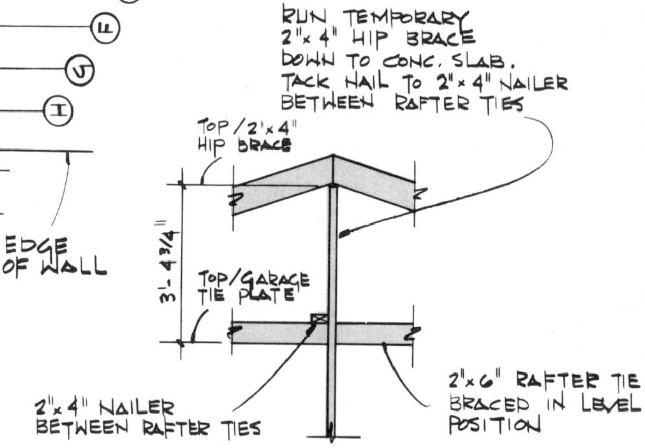

RUN TEMPORARY 2"x 4" HIP BRACE DOWN TO CONC. SLAB. TACK NAIL TO 2"x 4" NAILER BETWEEN RAFTER TIES
TOP / 2"x 4" HIP BRACE
3'- 4 3/4"
TOP/GARAGE TIE PLATE
2"x 4" NAILER BETWEEN RAFTER TIES
2"x 6" RAFTER TIE BRACED IN LEVEL POSITION

HIP RAFTER BRACING DETAIL "5B"

SCALE 3/8" = 1'-0"

JACK - RAFTER SCHEDULE																
POSITION	A	A'	B	B'	C	C'	D	D'	E	E'	F	F'	G	G'	H	J
OVER ALL LENGTH = "X"	12'-1"	13'-5 7/8"	10'-8 1/8"	12'-1"	9'-3 1/4"	10'-8 1/8"	7'-10 3/8"	9'-3 1/4"	6'-5 1/2"	7'-10 3/8"	5'-0 5/8"	6'-5 1/2"	3'-7 3/4"	5'-0 5/8"	2'-2 7/8"	4'-6"
NO. REQUIRED AT 45° BEVEL	3	1	3	1	3	1	3	1	3	1	3	1	3	1	4	1
NO. REQ'D AT REVERSE 45° B.	3	1	3	1	3	1	3	1	3	1	3	1	3	1	4	1

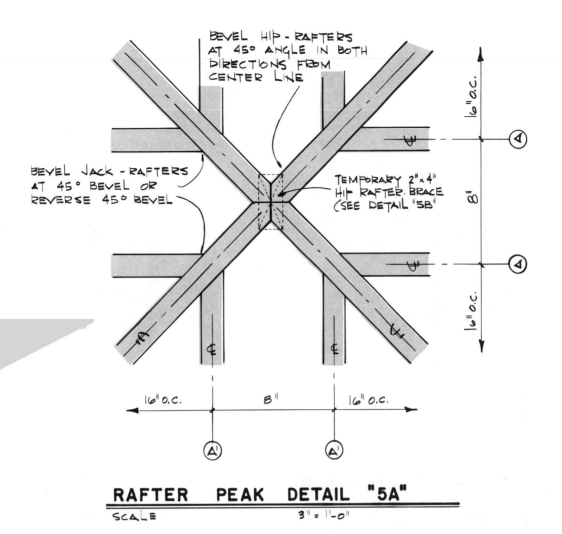

BEVEL HIP-RAFTERS AT 45° ANGLE IN BOTH DIRECTIONS FROM CENTER LINE

BEVEL JACK-RAFTERS AT 45° BEVEL OR REVERSE 45° BEVEL

TEMPORARY 2"x4" HIP RAFTER BRACE (SEE DETAIL "5B")

16" O.C.

8"

16" O.C.

16" O.C.   8"   16" O.C.

RAFTER   PEAK   DETAIL   "5A"

SCALE   3" = 1'-0"

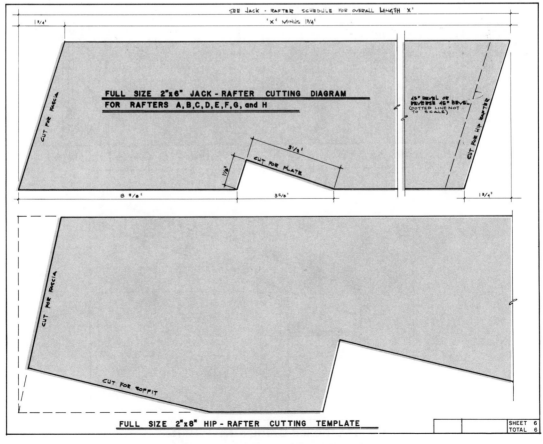

SEE JACK-RAFTER SCHEDULE FOR OVERALL LENGTH X'

1 3/4"   'X' MINUS 13/4"

FULL SIZE 2"x6" JACK-RAFTER CUTTING DIAGRAM FOR RAFTERS A,B,C,D,E,F,G, and H

CUT FOR FASCIA

45° BEVEL OR REVERSE 45° BEVEL (DOTTED LINE NOT TO SCALE)

CUT FOR HIP RAFTER

3 1/2"

11/8"

CUT FOR PLATE

8 5/8"   3 5/8"   1 3/4"

CUT FOR FASCIA

CUT FOR SOFFIT

FULL SIZE 2"x8" HIP-RAFTER CUTTING TEMPLATE

| | SHEET 6 |
| | TOTAL 6 |

Typical Hip Rafter Cutting Templates

43

EXTERIOR TRIM TREATMENTS

Before applying trim, know the nailing requirements of the siding you select. Some siding will have trim applied over the siding, other siding will butt against trim requiring extra blocking at edges. After the roof sheathing is on, but before you install the fascia and rake boards, add soffit nailers if required. Use the longest fascia boards on the longest walls.

Join all ends over the center of a rafter or nailer, Figure 44A–44E. At the gable end run the fasica (rake board) along the edge of roof sheathing and rafter. At top, cut the end to the angle of the rafter and butt at the center (prime coat ends with paint before butting). At lower end let front rake fascia extend beyond side fascia, then cut ends to line up with side fascia.

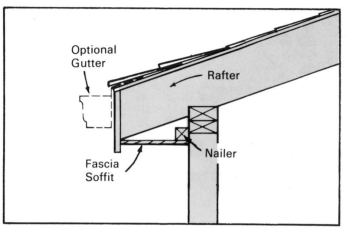

Figure 44A Boxed Cornice

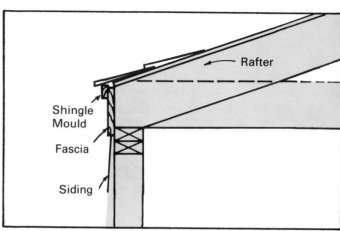

Figure 44B Cornice Detail

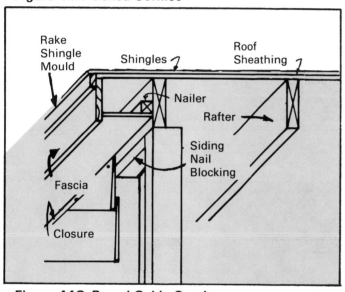

Figure 44C Boxed Gable Overhang

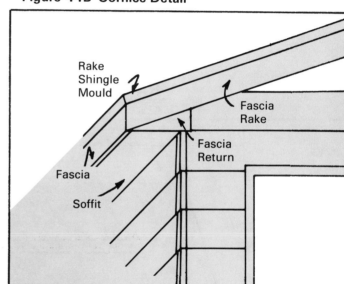

Figure 44D Gable End Detail

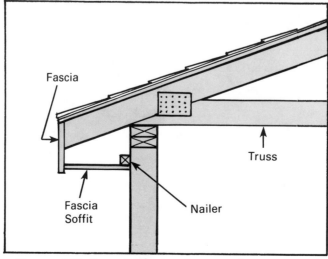

Figure 44E Boxed Cornice Truss Rafter

CORNER TRIM DETAILS

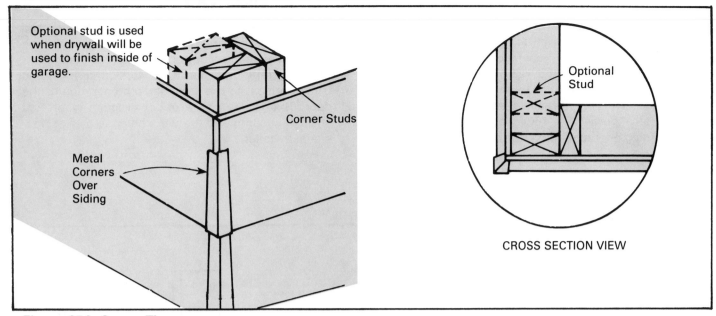

Optional stud is used when drywall will be used to finish inside of garage.

Corner Studs

Metal Corners Over Siding

Optional Stud

CROSS SECTION VIEW

Figure 45A Corner Tins

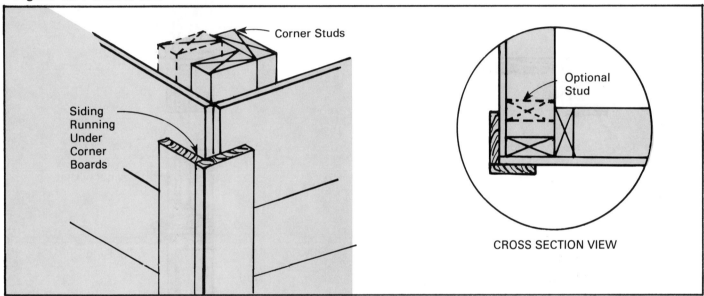

Corner Studs

Siding Running Under Corner Boards

Optional Stud

CROSS SECTION VIEW

Figure 45B Corner Boards

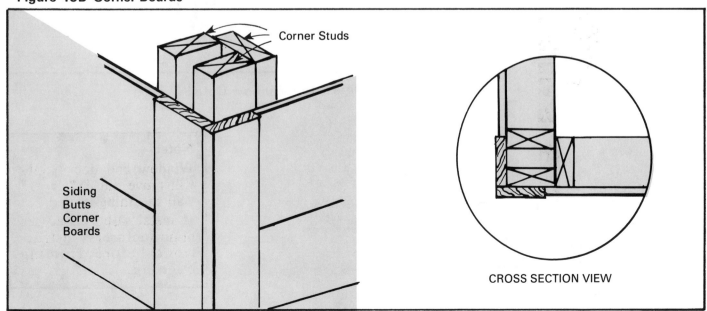

Corner Studs

Siding Butts Corner Boards

CROSS SECTION VIEW

Figure 45C Corner Boards

EXTERIOR TRIM CONTINUED

WINDOWS AND DOORS

Trim out door(s) as detailed on your garage plan. Because of the great variety in window manufacturing, it is best to study the window manufacturer's details before framing and trimming them. The service door to your garage can be ordered as a prehung door complete with threshold and side and head jambs. See Figures 46A–46C for construction details on trimming on-site window and door jambs.

GARAGE DOORS

Nail overhead doorjambs to the cripple studs and the header according to the directions given by the garage door manufacturer. The correct installation of garage door hardware, torsion springs, and trim is critical to the safe, smooth operation of the door. This is one phase of construction where we strongly recommend the work be done by a professional installer.

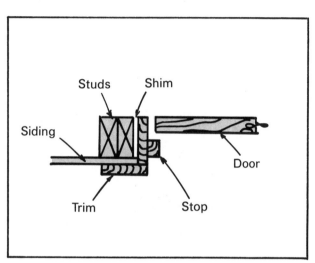

Figure 46A Door Detail

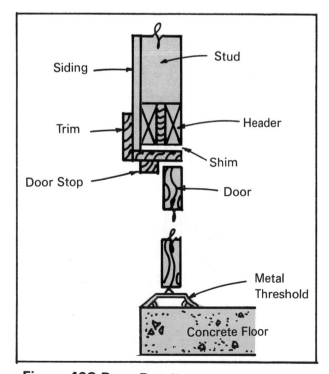

Figure 46C Door Detail

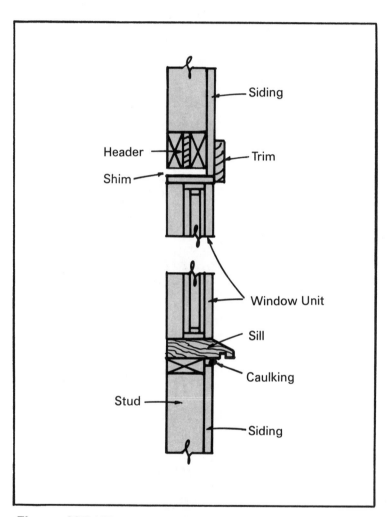

Figure 46B Window Detail

Note:
Window and door jambs will move out ½″ if ½″ wall sheathing is used.
If metal sash is used see manufacturers instructions before framing opening.

ROOF SHINGLES

Once the roof sheathing, cornice trim, and fascia boards are in place, the roof shingles can be applied. See shingle manufacturer's instructions on bundles. Shingles, chosen to harmonize with the home, are most popular. Square butt shingles are 36" × 12" in size, have three tabs, and are normally laid with 5" exposed to the weather (Figure 47A). Start with 15# asphalt felt paper at the bottom edge of the roof. Lap each course 2". After it is on, apply a starter course of shingles (shingles turned upside down), lapping over the eave and rake fascia 1/2" to provide a drip edge. Use four nails to each shingle: apply a Boston ridge at top, which is made by cutting a shingle into thirds (Figure 47B). Start at one end of the ridge and fasten with two nails to a shingle 5" exposure. Cut shingles with a utility knife. Metal drip edges are used in some locales.

When shingling a hip roof, a little more cutting is required. Use the hatchet gauge to give each hip shingle a 5" exposure.

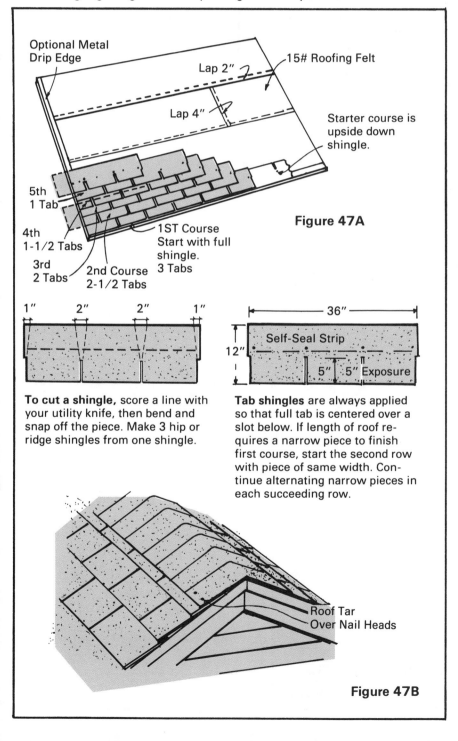

Optional Metal Drip Edge

Lap 2"

15# Roofing Felt

Lap 4"

Starter course is upside down shingle.

5th 1 Tab

4th 1-1/2 Tabs

3rd 2 Tabs

2nd Course 2-1/2 Tabs

1ST Course Start with full shingle. 3 Tabs

Figure 47A

1" 2" 2" 1"

36"

Self-Seal Strip

12"

5" 5" Exposure

To cut a shingle, score a line with your utility knife, then bend and snap off the piece. Make 3 hip or ridge shingles from one shingle.

Tab shingles are always applied so that full tab is centered over a slot below. If length of roof requires a narrow piece to finish first course, start the second row with piece of same width. Continue alternating narrow pieces in each succeeding row.

Roof Tar Over Nail Heads

Figure 47B

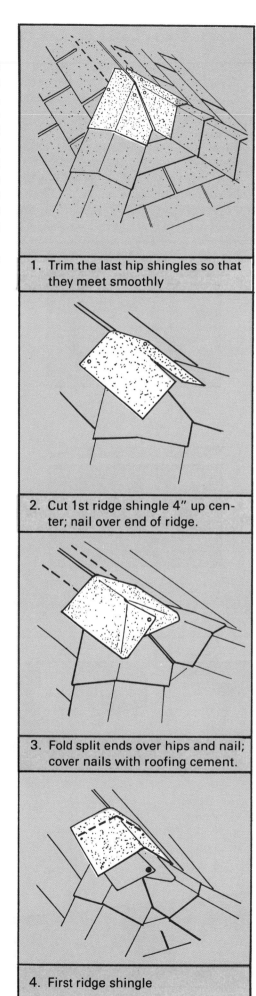

1. Trim the last hip shingles so that they meet smoothly

2. Cut 1st ridge shingle 4" up center; nail over end of ridge.

3. Fold split ends over hips and nail; cover nails with roofing cement.

4. First ridge shingle

EXTERIOR SIDING

Before starting construction, select the siding and determine the need for sheathing as it will involve the stud spacing, the width of the door and window jambs, and the application of the trim, Figures 46A to 46C. Some sidings require wall sheathing as a backer, for example, aluminum, horizontal hardboard over 24" o.c. stud spacing. Wood shingles require 3/8" plywood or 3/4" wood sheathing. Insulation board sheathing comes in 4' × 8' sheets, 1/2" thick

and is quickly applied. When sheathing is used, diagonal corner bracing often can be omitted. Decide if trim is to be applied on top of the siding or butted into it. If butted, apply trim first, then apply siding, Figures 45A to 45C. Before installing siding, apply aluminum foil-coated building felt (vapor barrier) on outside face of walls with bright side of foil toward the inside of the garage. Aluminum siding manufacturers provide instructions with their siding.

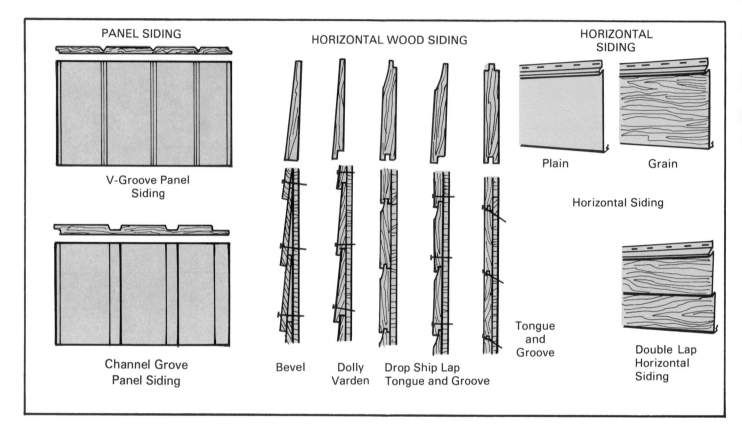

PANEL SIDING

V-Groove Panel Siding

Channel Grove Panel Siding

HORIZONTAL WOOD SIDING

Bevel

Dolly Varden

Drop Ship Lap Tongue and Groove

Tongue and Groove

HORIZONTAL SIDING

Plain

Grain

Horizontal Siding

Double Lap Horizontal Siding

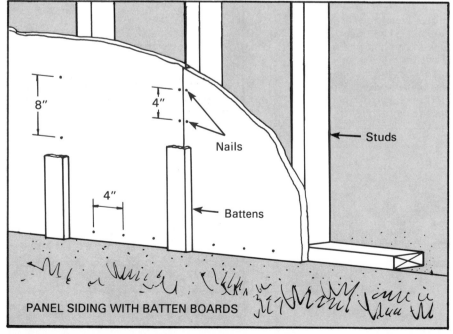

8"

4"

4"

Nails

Battens

Studs

PANEL SIDING WITH BATTEN BOARDS

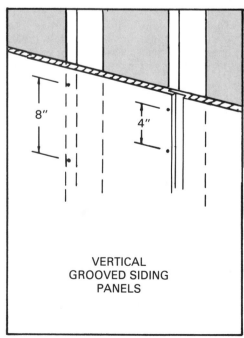

8"

4"

VERTICAL GROOVED SIDING PANELS

HORIZONTAL SIDING

Lay down various lengths of siding at each side. Apply so that joints in the succeeding course do not fall directly above each other. Butt all joints over the center of a stud. Seal (paint) edges of all siding before butting. Start 1/2" to 3/4" below the bottom plate. Siding on all walls should be aligned and level and each course equally spaced. Be especially careful to determine the lap and exposure to the weather before applying the second and succeeding courses. Measure the distance to be covered and divide it by the desired exposure to get the number of courses of siding, Figure 49B. Carefully mark these spaces on the corners of each wall, taking into consideration the overlap of the siding. Run a chalk line from one mark to another, leaving a horizontal chalk line on the building paper as a guide. Apply the siding, keeping it consistent by checking with your level.

Final openings, where siding meets the soffit (if any), can be closed with a quarter round or shingle mould. Protect your garage by painting or staining as soon as possible.

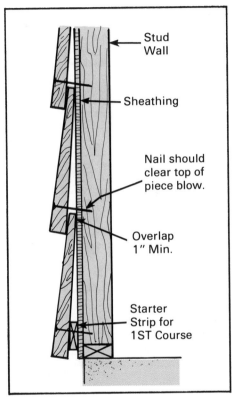

Figure 49A

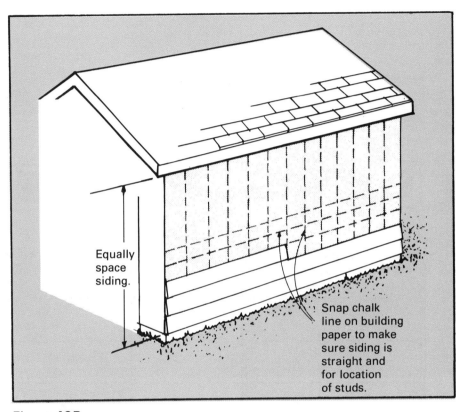

Figure 49B

BUILDING PAPER

Some local building codes might require that building paper be used to seal the wall from the elements. This is usually felt or kraft paper impregnated with asphalt that is stapled or nailed between the siding and the sheathing or studs. Rolls are 36" × 40" wide and come in lengths covering between 200 to 500 sq. ft. It is applied in horizontal strips from the bottom of the wall, Figure 49C. Overlaps are 2" at horizontal joints, 6" at vertical joints, and 12" at corners. Cutting is done with a utility knife. Use just enough staples or nails in installation to hold the paper in place; siding nails will hold it permanently. Also, before installing siding, a level chalk line should be snapped to indicate the bottom edge of the paper.

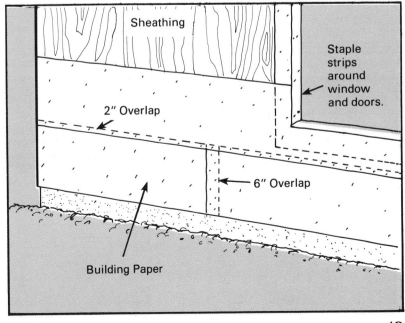

Figure 49C

GARAGE DOORS

The door is important. Due to the size of lots, building restrictions, and other reasons, the garage often takes an up-front position in visibility, in many cases its door is more prominent than the front door of the home. You will want a door that is compatible and attractive as well as utilitarian. There is a literal smorgasbord of styles and patterns from which to choose in today's market.

Governing factors are usually visual appeal and budget. The door can be as plain or as ornate as you wish. It can be made of wood, fiberglass, aluminum, or steel, and it can even be insulated with a poly core. It should be solid, constructed of materials that will stand a fair amount of hard use, and it should be lightweight and balanced so that even the youngsters in the family can operate it.

But most important are the headroom requirements and the doorjamb. If the jamb is improperly constructed, you will have nothing but grief with any door, no matter what type or quality. So, carefully check the specifications of the door manufacturer you select.

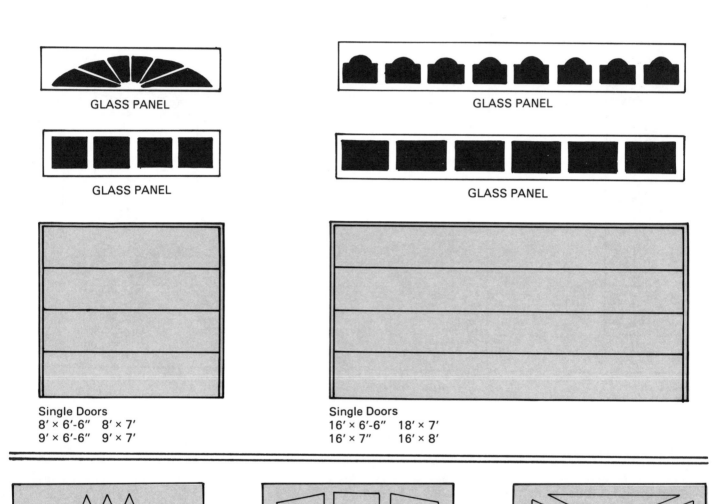

GLASS PANEL

GLASS PANEL

GLASS PANEL

GLASS PANEL

Single Doors
8′ × 6′-6″   8′ × 7′
9′ × 6′-6″   9′ × 7′

Single Doors
16′ × 6′-6″   18′ × 7′
16′ × 7″   16′ × 8′

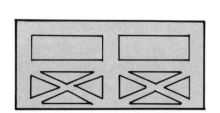

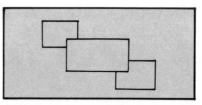

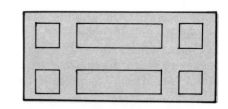

TYPICAL GARAGE DOOR DESIGNS

DOOR MOULDINGS

Moulding patterns and layout designs are almost as varied for garage doors as they are for the door to your house and are a great way to brighten up the front of the garage. The patterns shown here are just a suggestion of the many styles there are to choose from. Choose one or a combination of patterns, but keep in mind that the style and size of your door might affect the choice of moulding. What works on an upward-acting solid door might not work as well or look as good on a sectional or a side-acting door.

Remember that accurate measurements are important for mitering, especially since all the pieces should be cut to size before you're ready to attach them to the door. Also remember that the doors will be exposed to varied weather conditions, so they will need to be sealed, stained, or painted accordingly.

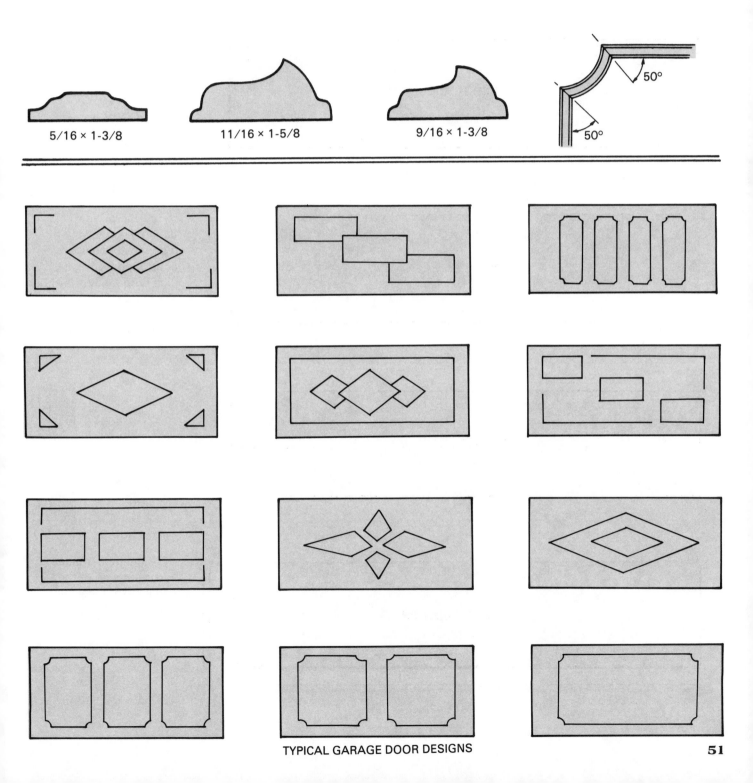

5/16 × 1-3/8   11/16 × 1-5/8   9/16 × 1-3/8   50°   50°

SECTIONAL GARAGE DOORS

Sectional garage doors are comprised of several horizontal sections held together with hinges. The side hinges have rollers so that the door section can roll up or down as a single unit. Rollers, track, and brackets are made to fit the sides and top of the door against the door frame for a snug weather-tight seal.

The bottom of the door should be weatherstripped. Standard rubber gasket stripping provides an especially tight fit.

Installation instructions for the door and its hardware are provided by the door manufacturer, but it is strongly recommended that this work be done by a professional. The torsion springs used to help lift and balance most door designs store tremendous amounts of energy and can cause severe bodily injury and/or property damage if accidentally released during installation or operation.

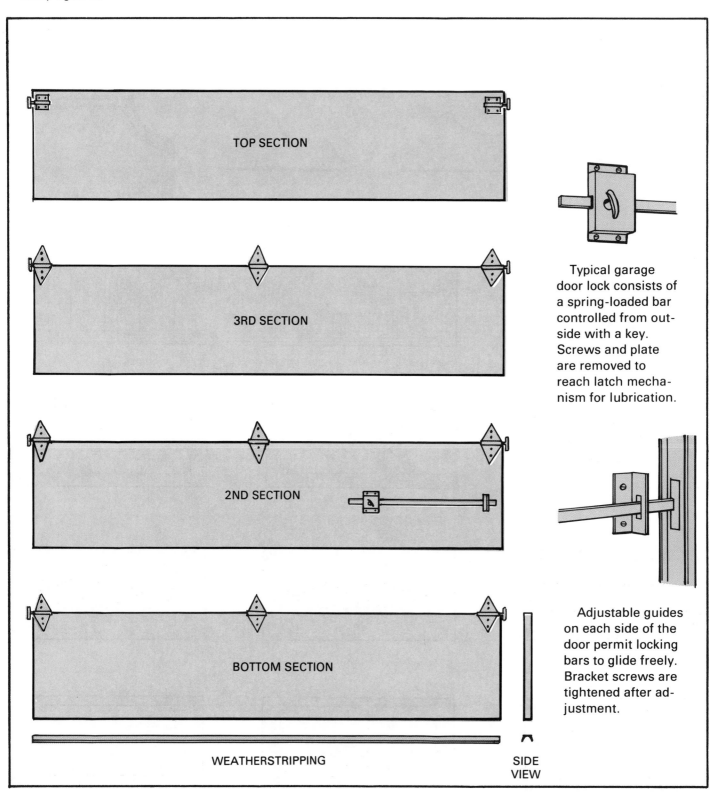

TOP SECTION

3RD SECTION

2ND SECTION

BOTTOM SECTION

WEATHERSTRIPPING

SIDE VIEW

Typical garage door lock consists of a spring-loaded bar controlled from outside with a key. Screws and plate are removed to reach latch mechanism for lubrication.

Adjustable guides on each side of the door permit locking bars to glide freely. Bracket screws are tightened after adjustment.

HARDWARE DETAILS

The torsion spring-type sectional door is operated by an assembly consisting of one or more torsion springs, a continuous torsion shaft, two lift drums, two lift cables, and associated hardware, including drum, torsion, shaft, torsion spring bearing, and bear-ing brackets. Track, roller bearings, and all hardware should be kept clean and lubricated. But as mentioned previously, all installation and adjustment of the system must be done by a professional.

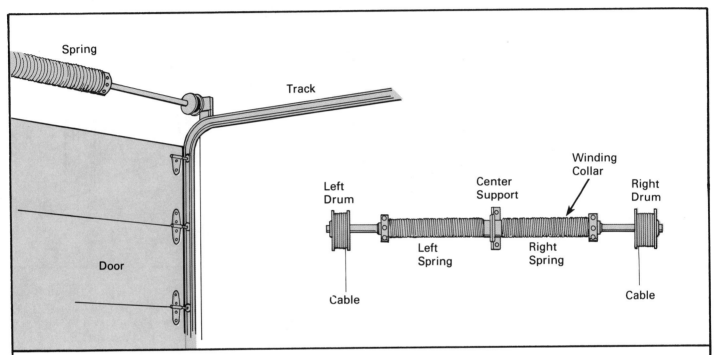

Garage door with single spring across door opening. This spring winds instead of stretching. Tension is adjusted by loosening the collar locknut and winding it tighter with a bar inserted through the collar.

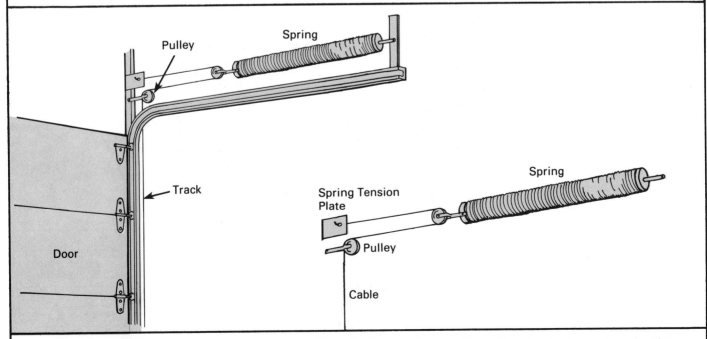

The door shown here has a spring on both sides. Spring tension is adjusted by shortening or lengthening the cable length at the spring tension plate.

INSTALLING PREHUNG DOOR

Prehung doors are assembled at the factory. The door comes hinged and mounted on the side jamb with a hole drilled through the door for the doorknob. A right-hand door or a left-hand door is determined by the side of the door on which the knob is located, viewed from inside the room into which it opens.

The door is installed by placing it into the rough opening and shimming it to make it square. Don't count on the opening being square.

After you've shimmed it so that the jamb is centered in the door opening, hold it in place by driving a 12d casing nail through the shims and into the trimmer stud near the top of the hinge-side jamb. Nail the head jamb to the header after making sure everything is square.

Again make sure the frame is centered and square, then

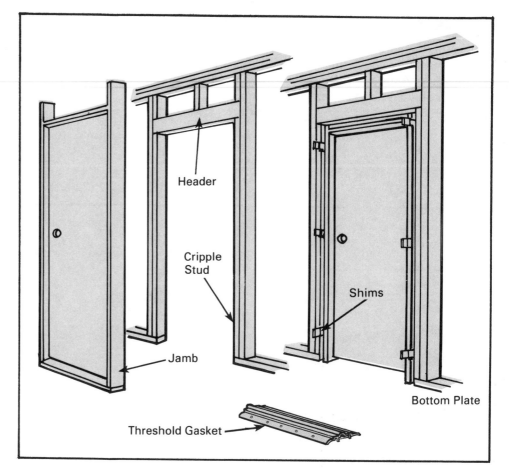

secure the hinge side by nailing into the trimmer stud through the shims. Check that the door swings freely, then secure the other jamb.

Weatherstripping is built into the threshold. The door must be removed to screw it to the existing threshold, and then measure and cut door to fit.

DISAPPEARING STAIRS

Folding stairways are factory-assembled for installation as a unit. The jamb is nailed to joists, and springs act as a counterbalance to the stairway and ceiling panel for easy operation. They are well suited to areas with limited head space, such as a garage loft, because the jambs and folded ladder use very little vertical space above the ceiling. Stair treads are normally painted with nonskid paint. Manufacturers provide installation instructions.

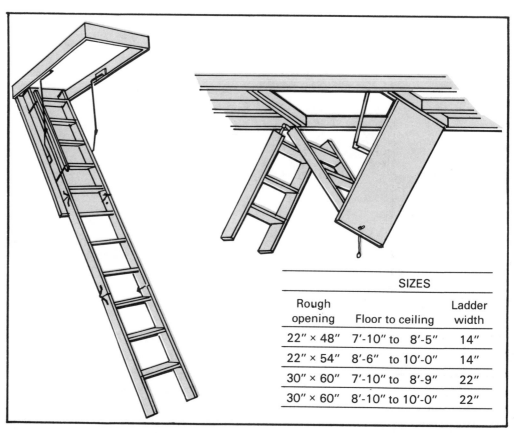

SIZES		
Rough opening	Floor to ceiling	Ladder width
22" × 48"	7'-10" to 8'-5"	14"
22" × 54"	8'-6" to 10'-0"	14"
30" × 60"	7'-10" to 8'-9"	22"
30" × 60"	8'-10" to 10'-0"	22"

BUILDING THE STAIRWAY

A stair assembly consists of stringers, risers, treads, and often railings. To build your stairs, begin by laying out the cut marks on the 2 × 12s to be used for stringers. Use a carpenter's square with the tread dimensions marked on the body of the square and the riser dimensions on the square tongue. Cuts can be made with either a handsaw or a circular saw, but final cut should be hand-made.

Remember that the bottom edge of the riser rests on the tread beneath it, while the forward edge of the tread is flush or overhangs the riser beneath it. A 1-1/8" overhang creates a professional look.

Cut out one stringer first and check its alignment. If it is correct, use it as a master for the second stringer. A third one will also need to be cut if the stairs are 36" wide or more.

Nail the top of the stringer to trimmers or header of the rough opening. For additional strength, an ex-

tra header board, a ledger, or joist hangers can be used. The bottoms are toenailed to the floor or to a 2 × 4 bottom ledger.

Attach treads first with 12d nails, then nail on the riser with 8d nails. Gluing the risers and treads to the stringers, along with nailing, will help reduce noise. Check local building code for stair construction.

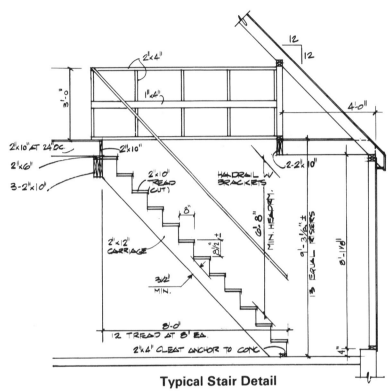

Typical Stair Detail

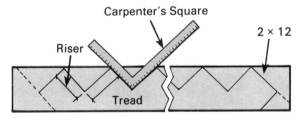

Laying Out A Stringer

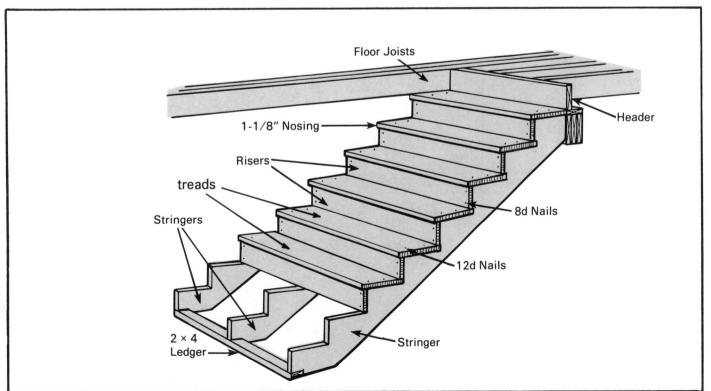

Typical Stairway

ELECTRICAL WIRING

If you plan on wiring your garage for electricity and are considering doing it yourself, two stops are almost mandatory: your local building code office and the power company, in that order. The code office will be able to inform you of any local wiring requirements, and they can be quite specific. They can also vary widely from one area to another. Don't bet on the code being exactly the same as it was in the last town you lived in. Even though many municipalities use the National Electrical Code (NEC), which spells out uniform safety standards for wiring methods and materials, it is often modified from one municipality to another to meet local needs. Checking with the code office can advise you of those variations, as well as setting you up on permit and inspection requirements. It will also advise you whether or not there are any requirements for using a professional electrician during the wiring. Remember that whether or not there are such requirements, if there's something that you're not sure of when you are putting in the wiring, it's best to have professional assistance.

The power company will be able to tell you the best or required location for a meter and service panel if the garage will be separately serviced. If you plan on running off existing home service, you can avoid trouble by making sure that the existing lines are able to carry the additional load.

Layout the location of all outlet boxes and lights on a floorplan of the garage to help in estimating material requirements. Plan on several outlets if you will use the garage as a workshop area, and be sure there is plenty of lighting for safety purposes. It is best to plan now to avoid headaches later. If you are installing an overhead garage door opener, you will also need a three-prong ceiling outlet placed in the proper position.

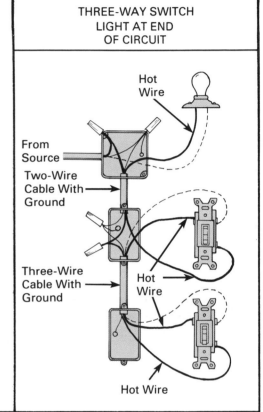

THREE-WAY SWITCH
LIGHT AT END
OF CIRCUIT

Hot Wire

From Source

Two-Wire Cable With Ground

Three-Wire Cable With Ground

Hot Wire

Hot Wire

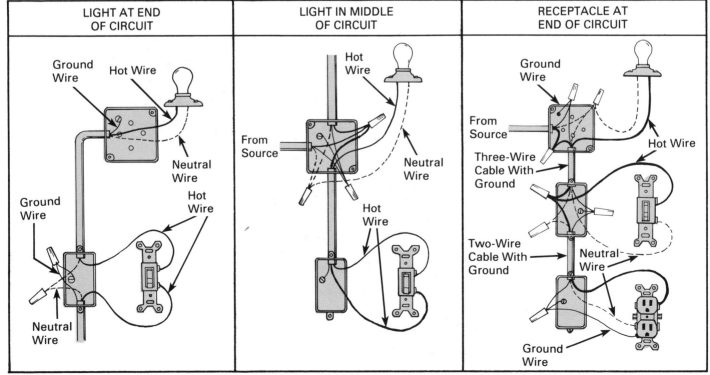

LIGHT AT END OF CIRCUIT

Ground Wire

Hot Wire

Neutral Wire

Ground Wire

Hot Wire

Neutral Wire

LIGHT IN MIDDLE OF CIRCUIT

Hot Wire

From Source

Neutral Wire

Hot Wire

RECEPTACLE AT END OF CIRCUIT

Ground Wire

From Source

Hot Wire

Three-Wire Cable With Ground

Two-Wire Cable With Ground

Neutral Wire

Ground Wire

　Typical Wiring Circuits

GARAGE DOOR OPENER

One of the most common garage accessories is the automatic garage door opener. It is available in a wide range of models from a number of manufacturers, generally at moderate expense and with a variety of features. Besides permitting you to open the garage door in stormy weather or at night without leaving the car, openers can provide interior garage lighting and a secure locking system.

Unlike the actual door and hardware, the opener itself is something you can easily install yourself. Carefully follow the manufacturer's instructions for mounting the opener at the correct height and securing it to the door header and the door.

Most openers offer a programmable remote control transmitter so you can personally select the radio frequency that opens your door. A separate wall-mounted switch is also a convenient feature to look for when selecting your opener.

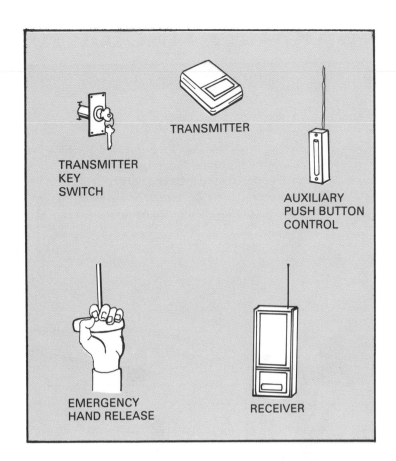

TRANSMITTER KEY SWITCH

TRANSMITTER

AUXILIARY PUSH BUTTON CONTROL

EMERGENCY HAND RELEASE

RECEIVER

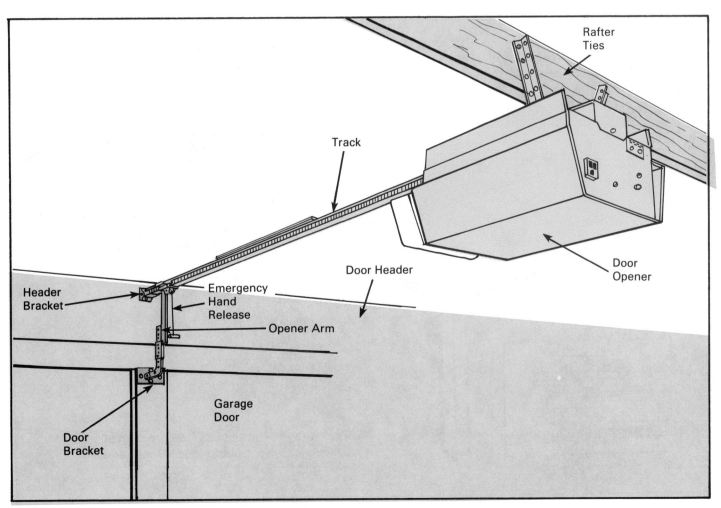

Rafter Ties

Track

Door Header

Door Opener

Header Bracket

Emergency Hand Release

Opener Arm

Garage Door

Door Bracket

GARAGE STORAGE IDEAS

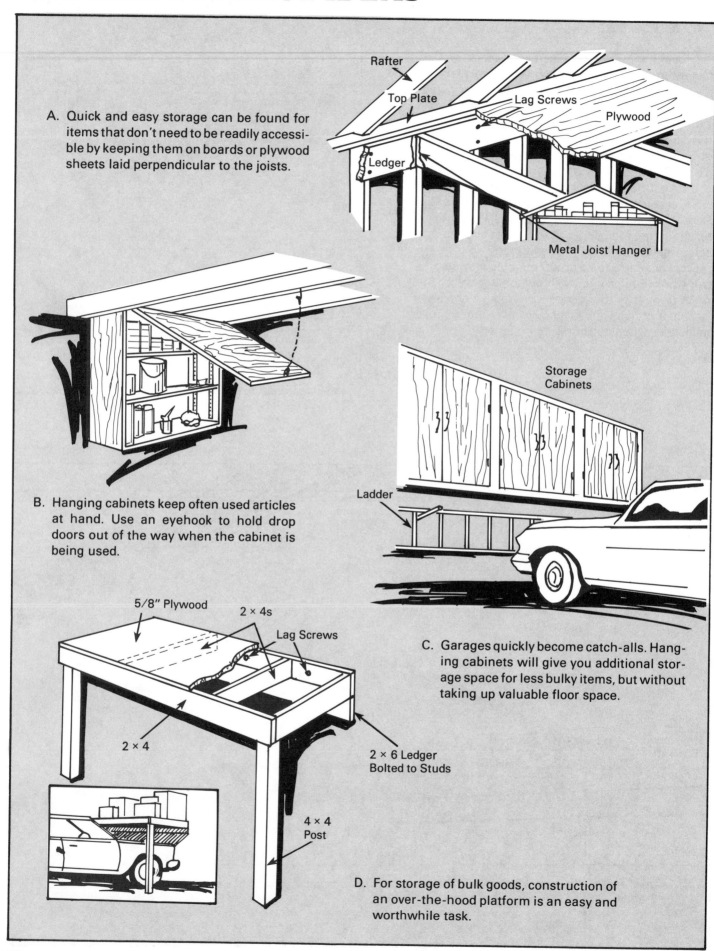

A. Quick and easy storage can be found for items that don't need to be readily accessible by keeping them on boards or plywood sheets laid perpendicular to the joists.

Rafter
Top Plate
Lag Screws
Plywood
Ledger
Metal Joist Hanger

B. Hanging cabinets keep often used articles at hand. Use an eyehook to hold drop doors out of the way when the cabinet is being used.

Storage Cabinets
Ladder

C. Garages quickly become catch-alls. Hanging cabinets will give you additional storage space for less bulky items, but without taking up valuable floor space.

5/8" Plywood
2 × 4s
Lag Screws
2 × 4
2 × 6 Ledger Bolted to Studs
4 × 4 Post

D. For storage of bulk goods, construction of an over-the-hood platform is an easy and worthwhile task.

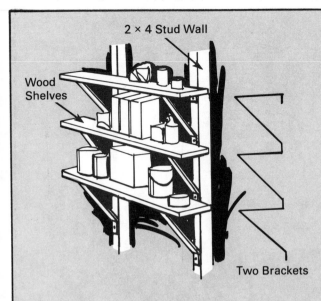

2 × 4 Stud Wall

Wood Shelves

Two Brackets

E. Smaller items can be stored on projecting shelves hung on studs or closed walls.

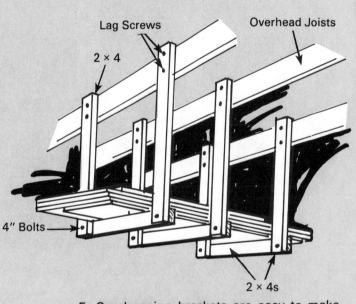

Lag Screws

Overhead Joists

2 × 4

4" Bolts

2 × 4s

F. Overhanging brackets are easy to make and offer out-of-the way storage for items such as lumber, pipes, etc.

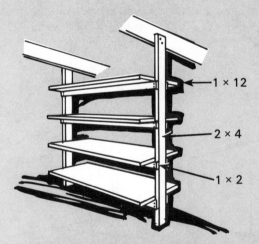

1 × 12

2 × 4

1 × 2

G. If you've got the space, deep shelves can be built quickly and simply with furring strips (1 × 2s), 2 × 4s, and plywood or 1 × 12s.

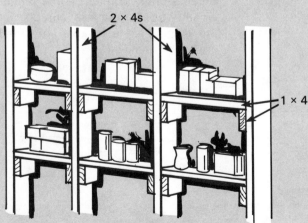

Overhead Joists

Lag Screws

2 × 4

Plywood Shelf

2 × 4

2 × 4

I. Be creative. One of a garage's big advantages is that there are very few set storage rules. A set-up like this that is made out of 2 × 4s and plywood gets not only the bikes out of the way, but other items as well.

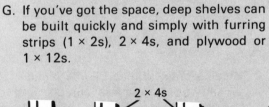

2 × 4s

1 × 4

H. Where space is tight, a couple of blocks nailed to the studs serve as good shelf supports. All you need is some 1 × 4s and you can build all the small-item storage you want.

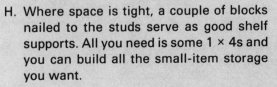

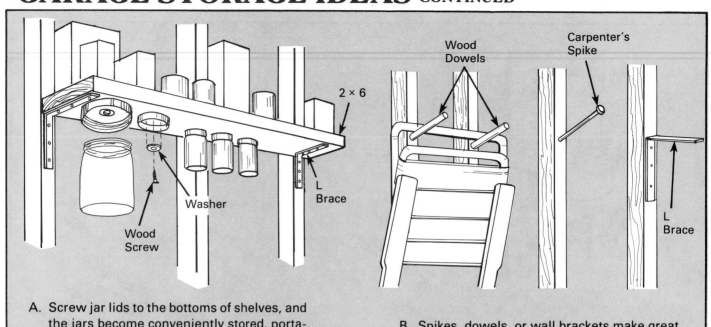

A. Screw jar lids to the bottoms of shelves, and the jars become conveniently stored, portable thingamabob containers.

B. Spikes, dowels, or wall brackets make great hangers on studs for many light items.

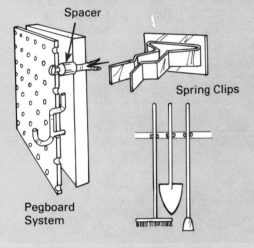

C. Pegboards and spring clips keep things visible, handy, and produce a tidy, organized effect.

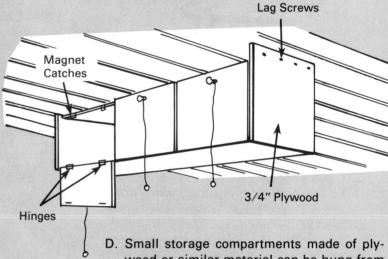

D. Small storage compartments made of plywood or similar material can be hung from the ceiling joists to keep seasonal items organized and clean.

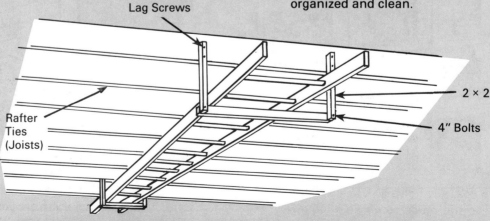

E. You've got to put a ladder somewhere. The garage is long enough, so hang it from the ceiling rather than leaving it on the floor where somebody is bound to trip over it or knock it down.

NATIONAL PLAN SERVICE PROJECT PLANS AVAILABLE

Plans for these do-it-yourself projects come complete with large, professional, easy-to-follow blueprints. There is also a complete list of materials needed and precise dimensional drawings for every detail.

To order the blueprints for these handy do-it-yourself projects, use the order form in the back of this book.

DO-IT-YOURSELF DESIGN
B50396
Work Table and Cabinet

This practical worktable and cabinet gives the perfect answers to storing all your tools—with lots of space to do work on any size job! Includes 2 patterns. **Table:** 6' wide × 36" deep × 36" high. **Cabinet:** 51" wide × 36" deep × 24" high.

DO-IT-YOURSELF DESIGN
B50065
Wired Workbench

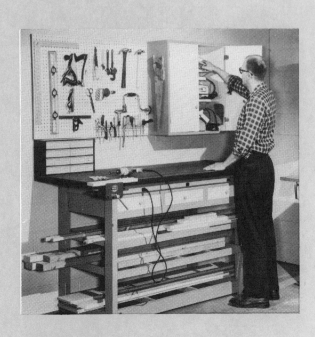

Drawers under bench top store small hand tools, while tool board and cabinet take charge of larger tools and power tools. Size can be adapted to your specific needs.

DO-IT-YOURSELF DESIGN
B2040
Two Cupolas

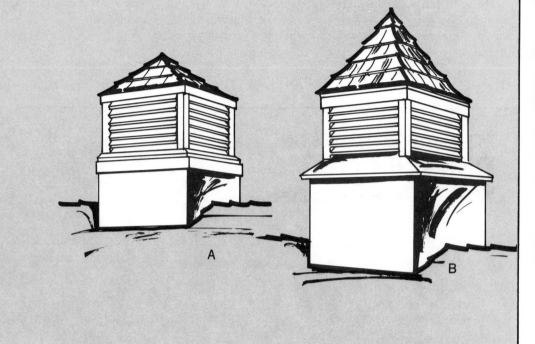

- Sizes
  A—30″ × 30″ × 40″ H
  B—33″ × 33″ × 60″ H
- A decorative finishing touch for your garage
- Easy to build

DO-IT-YOURSELF DESIGN
B2052
Workbench

- This practical workbench has a very unique feature...a mobile tool caddy that rolls out from under the workbench for added workspace.
- Perfect for storing tools.
- Enough work space to handle those larger projects.
- Size: 30-1/2″ × 6′-0″ × 40″ H

READY TO START SERIOUS PLANNING?

Now that you have read this book from cover to cover, you're ready to start serious planning. As you can see, there are many details to consider, and they all seem to tie together.

If the procedures appear a little confusing, reread the information outlined in this book several times before deciding which phases of the construction you want to handle yourself and which you might want to rely on professional assistance. For example, you may wish to have the concrete foundation work done by a professional and handle the framing and finishing work yourself.

Because drawing up your own plan from scratch can be time consuming and difficult for the inexperienced, you might want to make planning and cost estimating easier by selecting a design from those shown in this book. If blueprints with lumber lists are not immediately available from your building material dealers, you can order them. Use the order form in the back of this book. If after reviewing the blueprints you still have questions, talk them over with your lumber dealer. Most dealers are familiar with construction and glad to help.

The following 21 pages include an assortment of garage plans, garage apartments, and pole buildings.

Construction blueprints can be obtained by using the order form in the back of this book.

All blueprint plans include exterior elevations, sections and details, floor plans, foundation plans, rafter templates, and lumber lists.

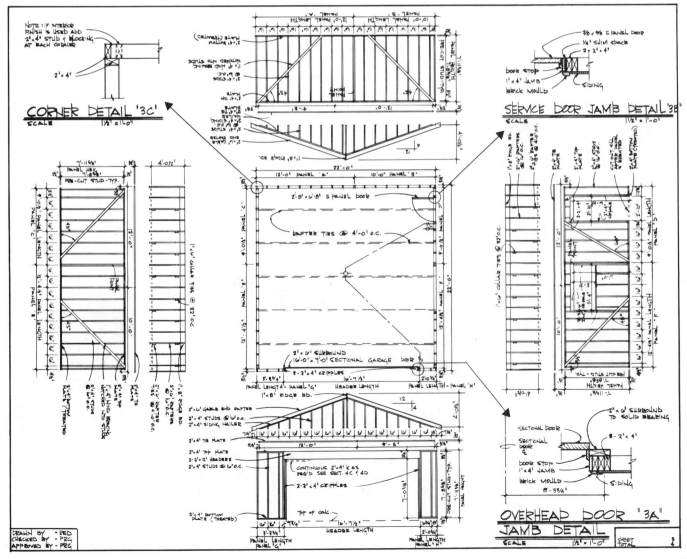

DESIGNS FOR GARAGES, GARAGE APARTMENTS AND POLE BUILDINGS...

Complete blueprint plans are available for all the following garage and pole building designs... <u>See order form in back of this book.</u>

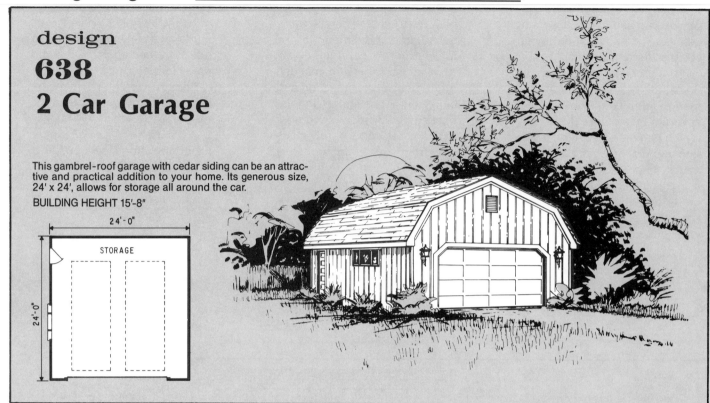

design
638
2 Car Garage

This gambrel-roof garage with cedar siding can be an attractive and practical addition to your home. Its generous size, 24' x 24', allows for storage all around the car.

BUILDING HEIGHT 15'-8"

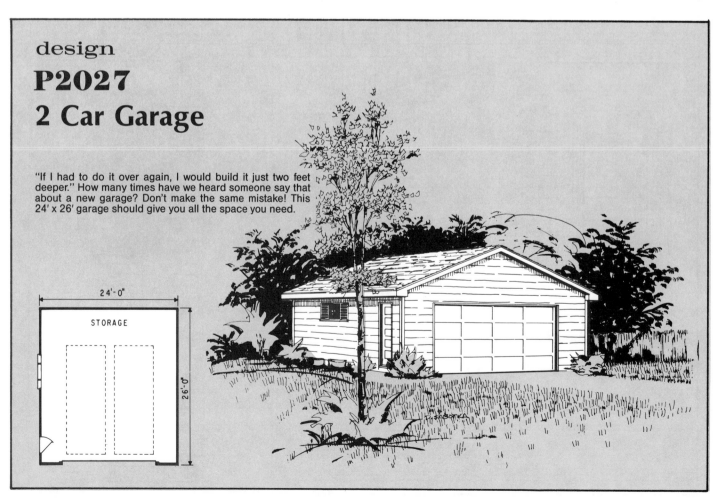

design
P2027
2 Car Garage

"If I had to do it over again, I would build it just two feet deeper." How many times have we heard someone say that about a new garage? Don't make the same mistake! This 24' x 26' garage should give you all the space you need.

design

P2012

2 Car Garage

A 24' x 24' garage that makes maximum use of space. The off-center garage door allows for storage or workbench space on the one side. The 24' depth will also leave space at the rear for additional storage.

design

P2017

2 Car Garage

SIZE 22' x 22'

design

642

2 Car Garage

SIZE 20' x 20'

A basic garage. This design is available in two sizes, but regardless of which size you choose it will be an added asset to your property.

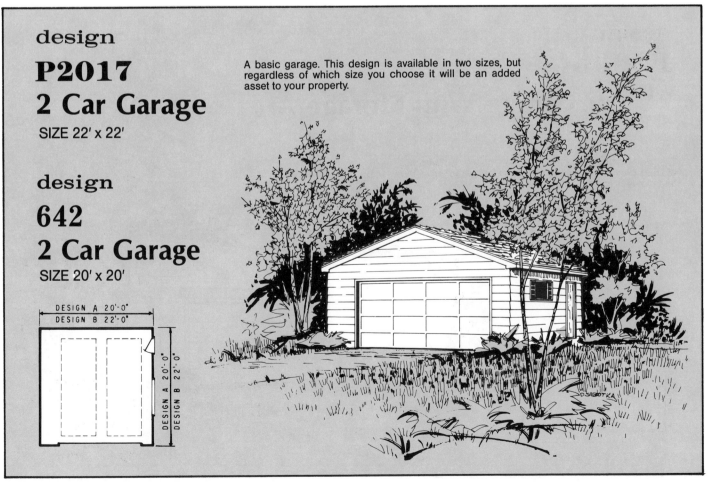

design

643
2 Car Garage

An attractive garage with his and hers overhead doors. This design also gives you added storage space beyond the two cars.

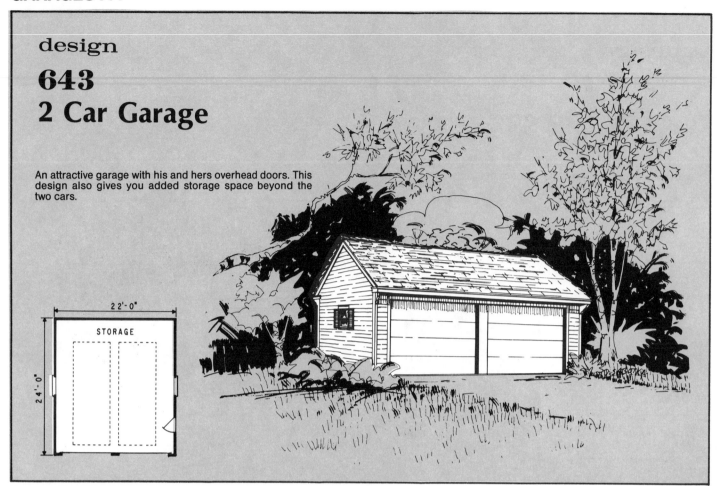

STORAGE

2 2'-0"

2 4'-0"

design

P2006

2½ Car Garage With Storage Area

This double-duty garage will not only house two cars but will also provide you with ample space for a large workshop and plenty of room for storage.

30'

619

22'

STORAGE

design
P2013
1 Car Garage With Storage Area and Covered Porch

This two-in-one garage allows generous space for one car with space left over for storage. The covered porch will provide you a shady outdoor sitting area on those hot summer days.

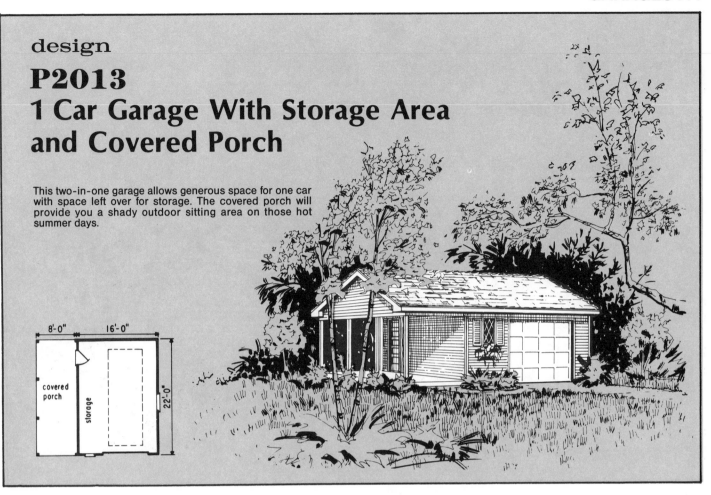

design
P2015
1½ Car Garage With Storage

If all you need is a one-car garage plus some storage space this 14' x 22' garage is just what you have been looking for. The overhead door is offset to allow extra storage and work-bench space on the one side.

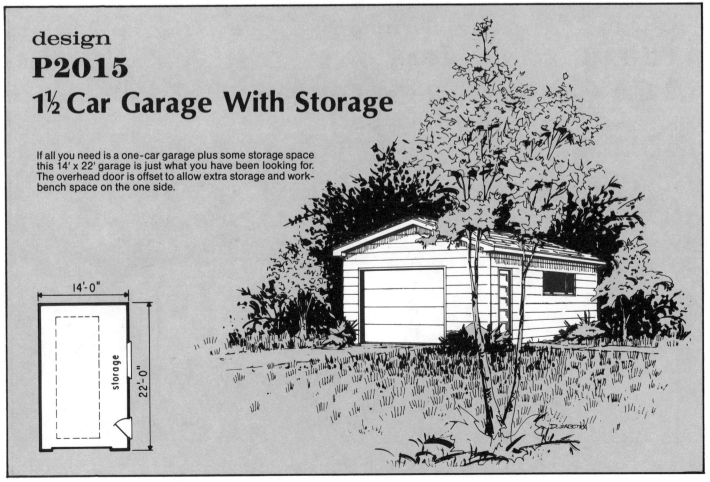

design
P2010
2 Car Garage

This attractive colonial design with panel doors and high pitch roof make this an ideal two-car garage to add to any colonial or traditional home.

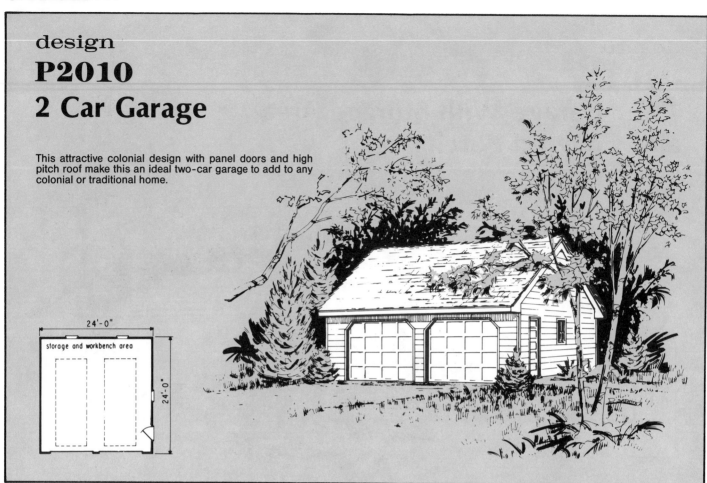

24'-0"

storage and workbench area

24'-0"

design
P2016
2 Car Garage

SIZE 22' x 22'
Design A – 20' x 20'
Design B – 22' x 22'

design
648
2 Car Garage

SIZE 20' x 20'

Here's an attractive hip-roof design that will look good on any lot. The extended roof over the garage door affords it protection from the weather.

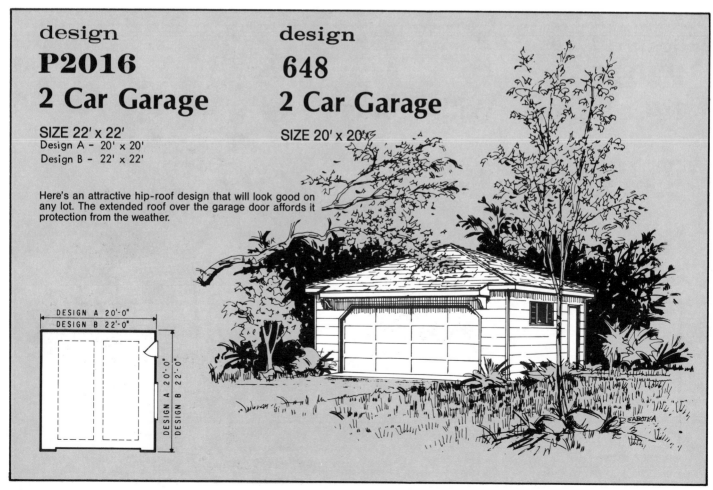

DESIGN A 20'-0"
DESIGN B 22'-0"

DESIGN A 20'-0"
DESIGN B 22'-0"

design

633

2 Car Garage ... Build it Freestanding or Attached

Plans are drawn so you can either add this traditionally-styled garage to your existing home . . . or build it detached. The convenient service doors afford access to the storage side from the front or rear.

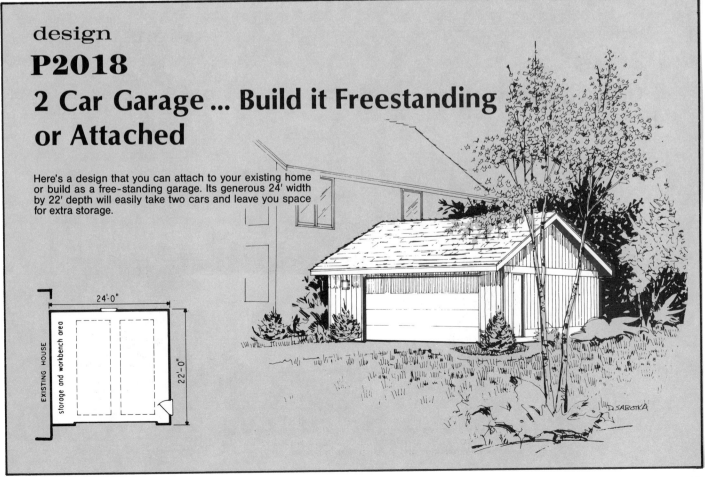

design

P2018

2 Car Garage ... Build it Freestanding or Attached

Here's a design that you can attach to your existing home or build as a free-standing garage. Its generous 24' width by 22' depth will easily take two cars and leave you space for extra storage.

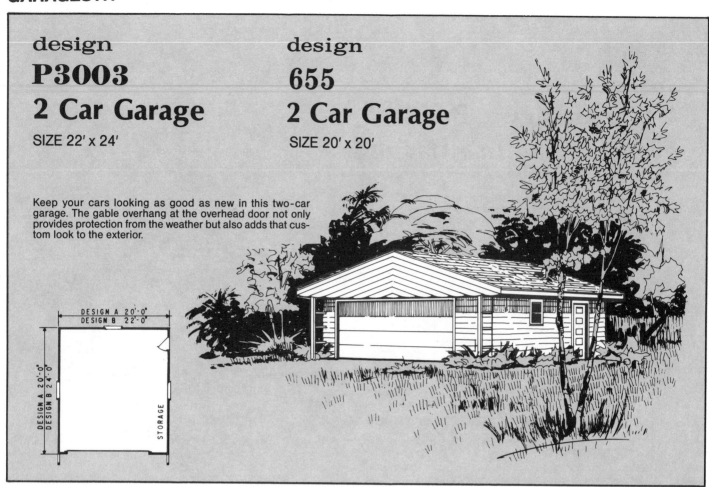

design
P3003
2 Car Garage
SIZE 22' x 24'

design
655
2 Car Garage
SIZE 20' x 20'

Keep your cars looking as good as new in this two-car garage. The gable overhang at the overhead door not only provides protection from the weather but also adds that custom look to the exterior.

DESIGN A 20'-0"
DESIGN B 22'-0"

DESIGN A 20'-0"
DESIGN B 24'-0"

STORAGE

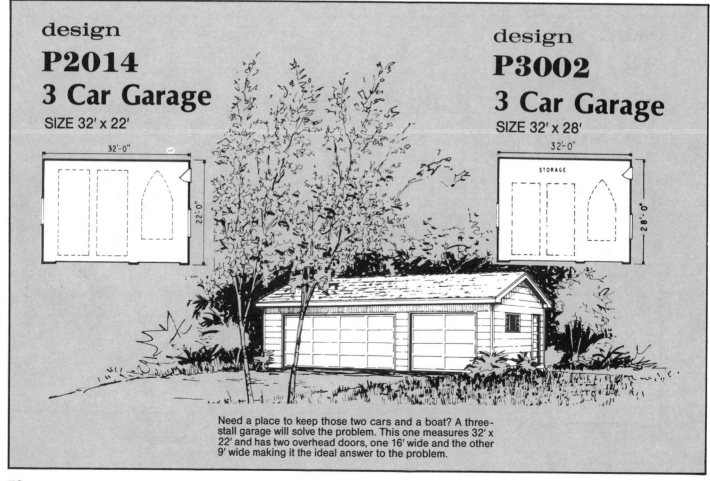

design
P2014
3 Car Garage
SIZE 32' x 22'

32'-0"

22'-0"

design
P3002
3 Car Garage
SIZE 32' x 28'

32'-0"

STORAGE

28'-0"

Need a place to keep those two cars and a boat? A three-stall garage will solve the problem. This one measures 32' x 22' and has two overhead doors, one 16' wide and the other 9' wide making it the ideal answer to the problem.

design
657

2 Car Garage With Greenhouse

The 24' x 24' two-car garage would by itself be a valued addition to your property. But this one will also allow you to let your green thumb show. The attached greenhouse has two jalousie sash and a gravel covered dirt floor making it an ideal spot for plant growth.

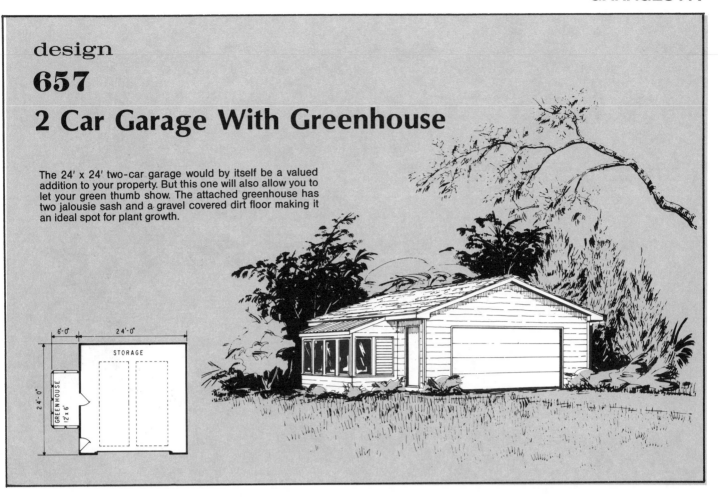

design
P2011

2 Car Garage With Storage Area

Double garage 24' wide by 24' deep will house two cars plus that lawn care equipment with space left to add the workbench you always wanted.

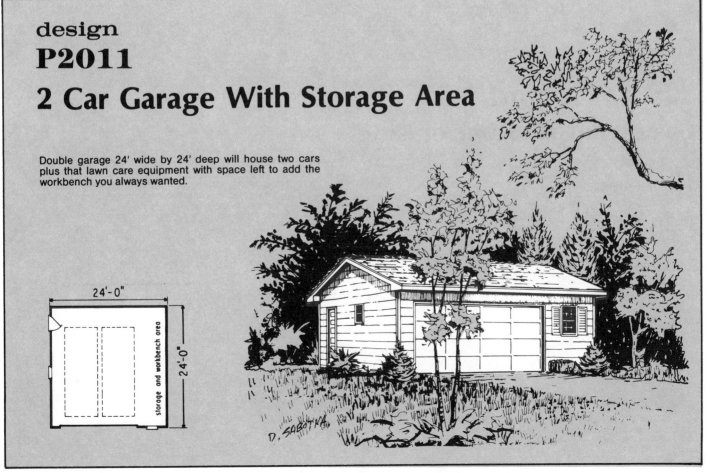

design
659
2 Car Garage

A functional two-car garage. It will provide the extra storage space most people need. The porch-like roof projection with arched frieze board adds charm and protection for the doors.

design
679
2 Car Carport With Storage
...Enter from front or side

This well-designed carport provides plenty of space for two cars plus two enclosed storage areas. The side door allows entry of long items such as extension ladders, long handled pruning cutters, etc. The unique design allows cars to enter from the front or side of carport.

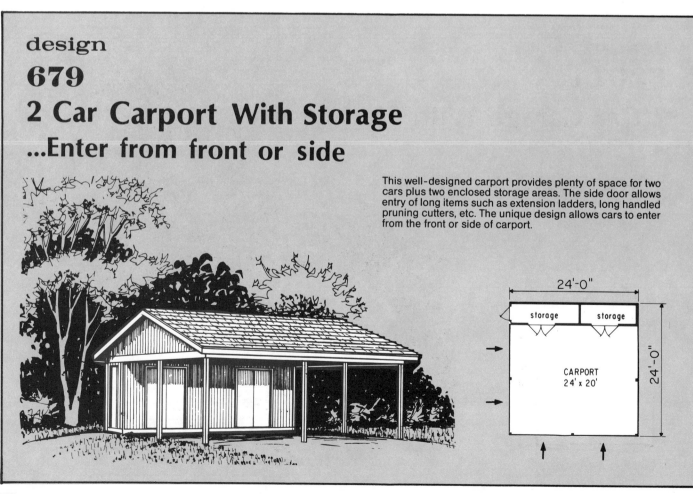

design
660
2 Car Garage With Storage

A helpful addition to your home. This 26' x 22' garage will house two cars and provide you two separate lockable storage compartments, one of which is accessible from the outside.

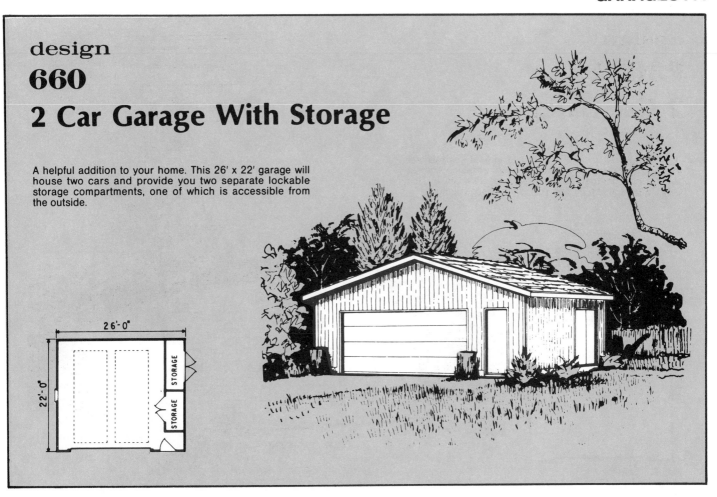

design
663 Salt Box
2 Car Garage With Storage

A helpful addition to your home . . . a "Salt-Box"-styled garage that provides the additional storage space we are all looking for.

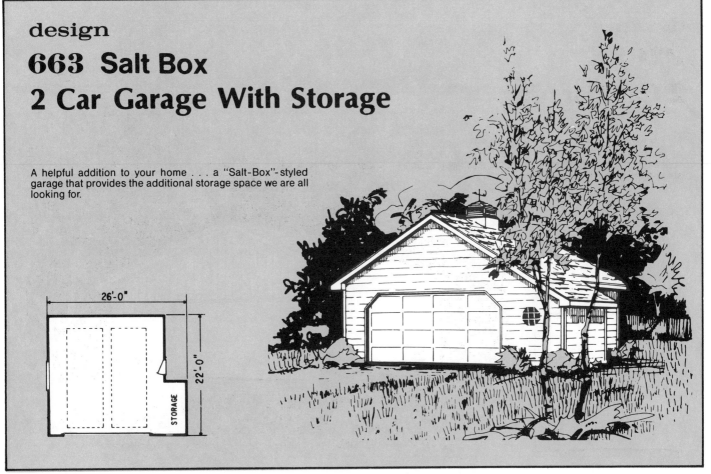

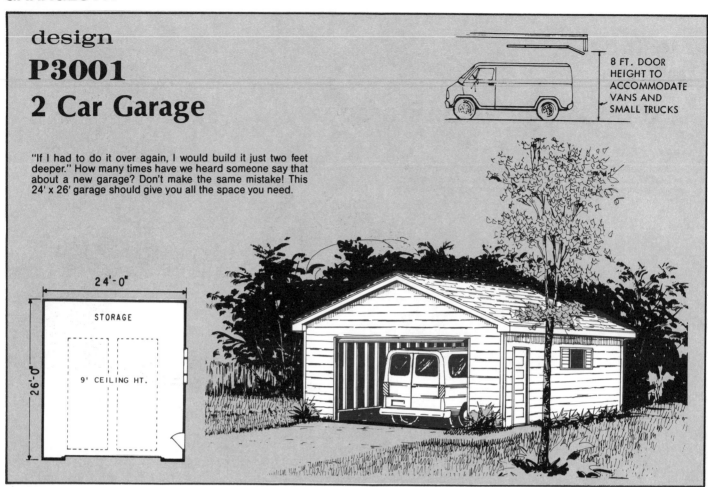

design
P3001
2 Car Garage

8 FT. DOOR HEIGHT TO ACCOMMODATE VANS AND SMALL TRUCKS

"If I had to do it over again, I would build it just two feet deeper." How many times have we heard someone say that about a new garage? Don't make the same mistake! This 24' x 26' garage should give you all the space you need.

24'-0"

STORAGE

9' CEILING HT.

26'-0"

design
P2026
2 Car Garage

A 24' x 24' garage that makes maximum use of space. The off-center garage door allows for storage or workbench space on the one side. The 24' depth will also leave space at the rear for additional storage.

24'-0"

24'-0"

storage and workbench area

D. SABOTKA

design
669
2 Car Garage

Keep your cars looking as good as new in this two car garage. The overhang at the overhead doors not only will provide protection from the weather but also adds that custom look to the exterior.

design
670
2½ Car Garage/Roadside Stand

Here is a garage designed for homeowners and also farmers and commercial users. This building provides an excellent showcase for selling farm-grown produce. There is a 6 foot cantilevered overhang across the front of the building and plenty of storage and display area.

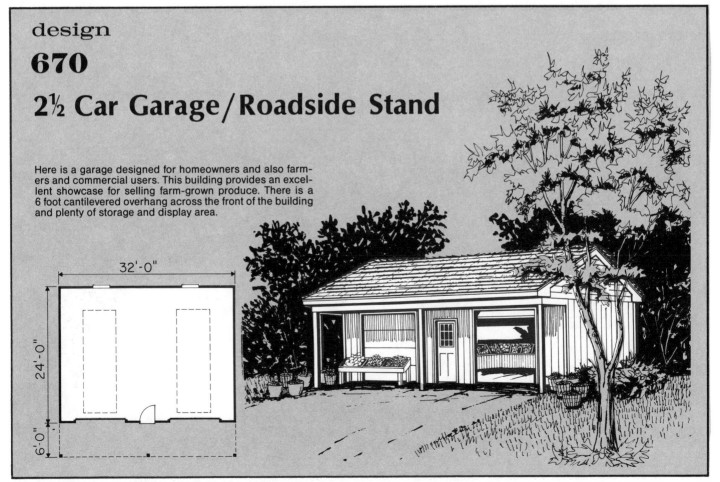

design
671
3 Car Garage/ Workshop

More than just a garage! This extra big 24' x 36' garage features three 9' wide x 8' high doors and boasts a 10' high ceiling. An ideal size for many applications such as a farm repair shop, contractor's garage, maintenance building, bicycle repair shop, general storage building, etc.

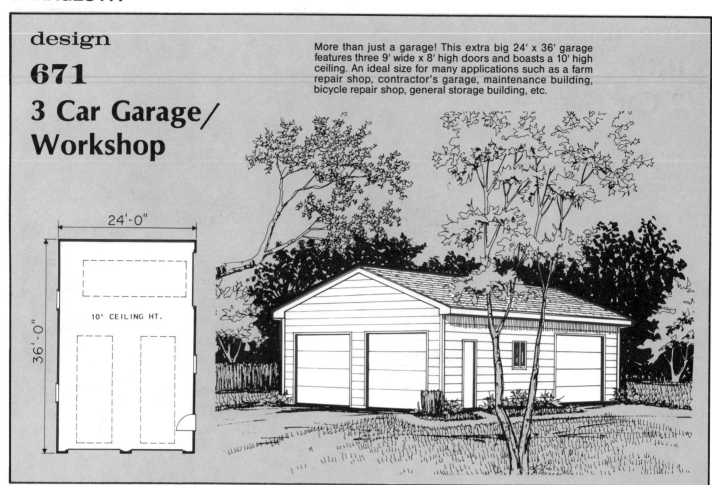

design
P2005
2 Car Garage With Studio Loft

Instead of building just a garage, why not build one that will serve triple duty? A two-car garage with workshop or hobby center and a loft that can be used as a studio or office are features that many homeowners are looking for.

BUILDING HEIGHT 21'-0"

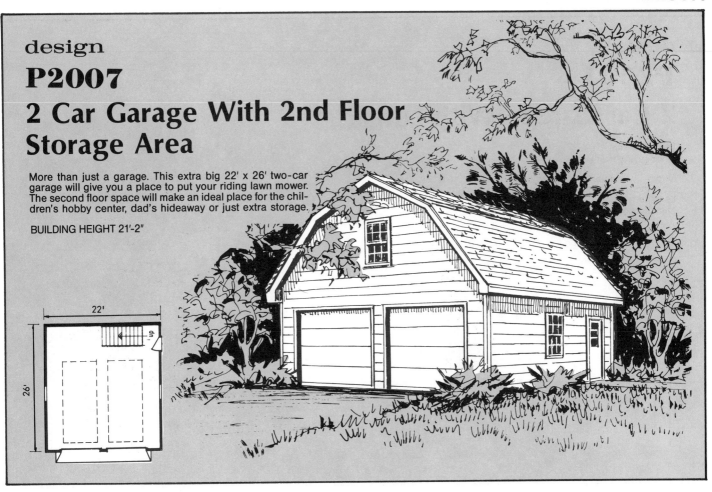

design
P2007
2 Car Garage With 2nd Floor Storage Area

More than just a garage. This extra big 22' x 26' two-car garage will give you a place to put your riding lawn mower. The second floor space will make an ideal place for the children's hobby center, dad's hideaway or just extra storage.

BUILDING HEIGHT 21'-2"

22'

26'

design
P2024
2 Car Garage With Loft

LOFT AREA

10'-3"

4'-4"

8'-1"

CROSS SECTION

Designed to fit the contemporary home style, this two-car garage has a 300-sq.-ft. loft area with a sloped roof running from a 4'-high wall at the rear to a 9½'-high wall at its front. It can make a good hide-a-way studio or just plain storage space.

BUILDING HEIGHT 20'-8"

26'-0"

STORAGE

24'-0"

UP

design
P2501

2 Car Garage With Loft

BUILDING HEIGHT 21'-3"
LOFT SIZE 27'-4" x 18'-8"

Originally designed with attractive dormers to give a colonial look, this design is also attractive if you omit the dormers. Its generous size provides plenty of storage. The loft is an ideal hobby area.

design
672

1 Car Garage With Loft

If all you need is a one car garage plus a lot of storage space, this 16' x 24' garage is just what you have been looking for! A staircase leads you up to the huge second floor storage loft which can also make an ideal place for the children's hobby center or Dad's hide-a-way.

BUILDING HEIGHT 19'-4"

design
673

3 Car Garage With Loft

Need a place to keep those two cars and a boat? A three stall garage will solve the problem. This one measures 36' x 24' and has three overhead doors, all 9' wide x 7' high, making it the ideal answer to the problem. A stairway leads to the second floor loft area. It can make a good hide-a-way studio or just plain storage space.

BUILDING HEIGHT 21'-4"

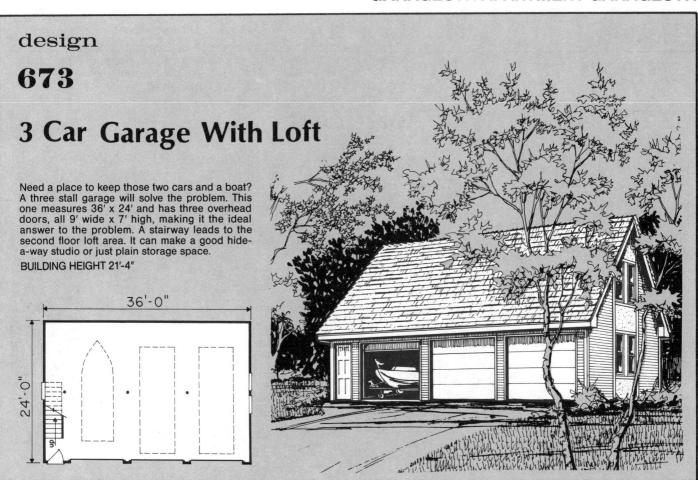

design
X6006

2 Car Garage With Apartment

When thinking of adding a garage, think about adding income to your property. This large two-car garage with a 764-sq.-ft. apartment above is certain to enhance your property and your income.

BUILDING HEIGHT 22'-6"

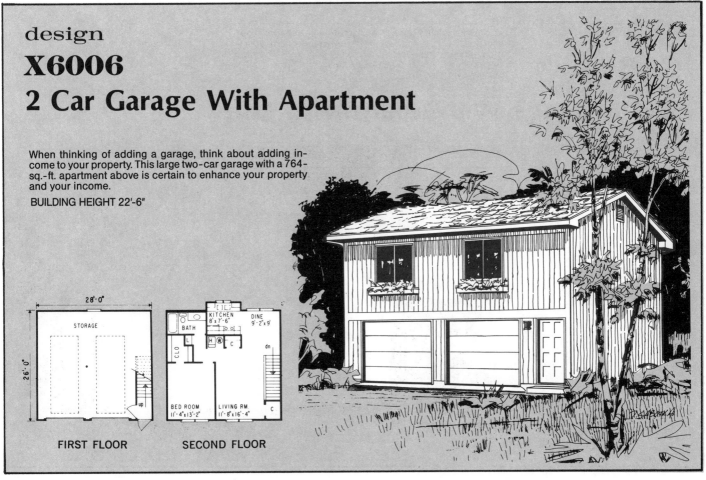

FIRST FLOOR   SECOND FLOOR

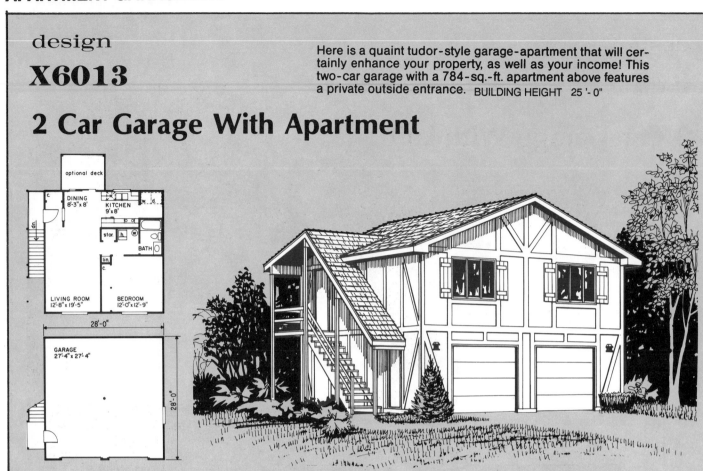

design
X6013

Here is a quaint tudor-style garage-apartment that will certainly enhance your property, as well as your income! This two-car garage with a 784-sq.-ft. apartment above features a private outside entrance. BUILDING HEIGHT 25'-0"

2 Car Garage With Apartment

optional deck

DINING 8'-3" x 8'

KITCHEN 9' x 8'

stor.

BATH

lin.

LIVING ROOM 12'-8" x 19'-5"

BEDROOM 12'-0" x 12'-9"

28'-0"

GARAGE 27'-4" x 27'-4"

28'-0"

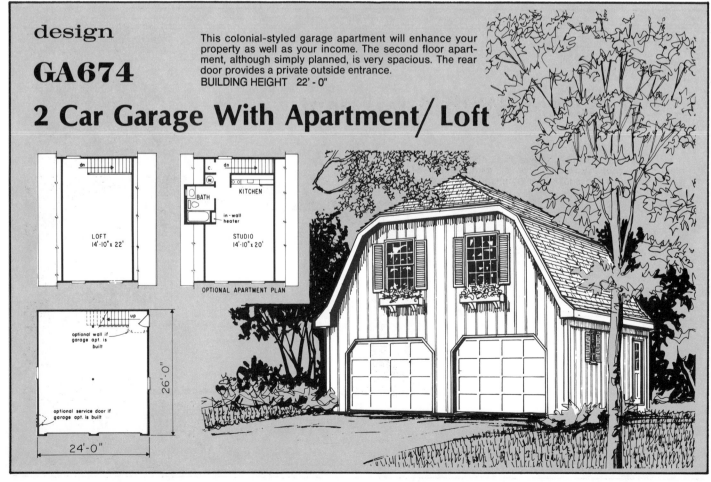

design
GA674

This colonial-styled garage apartment will enhance your property as well as your income. The second floor apartment, although simply planned, is very spacious. The rear door provides a private outside entrance.
BUILDING HEIGHT 22'-0"

2 Car Garage With Apartment/Loft

LOFT 14'-10" x 22'

BATH

KITCHEN

in-wall heater

STUDIO 14'-10" x 20'

OPTIONAL APARTMENT PLAN

optional wall if garage apt. is built

up

optional service door if garage apt. is built

26'-0"

24'-0"

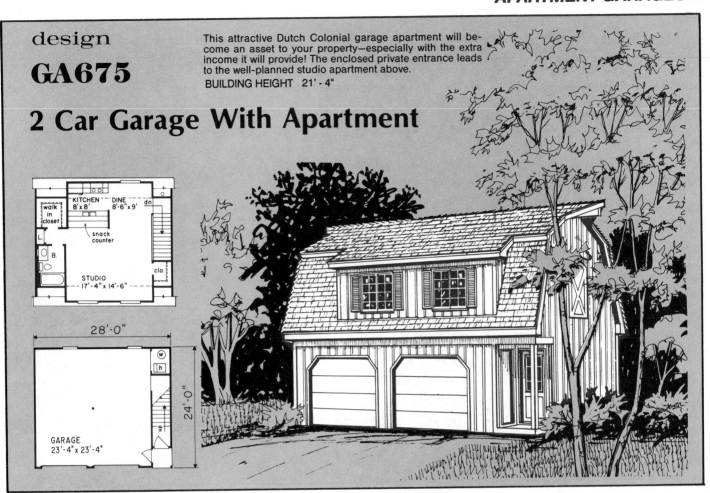

design

GA675

This attractive Dutch Colonial garage apartment will become an asset to your property—especially with the extra income it will provide! The enclosed private entrance leads to the well-planned studio apartment above.
BUILDING HEIGHT 21'-4"

2 Car Garage With Apartment

KITCHEN 8' x 8'
DINE 8'-6" x 9'
walk in closet
dn
snack counter
STUDIO 17'-4" x 14'-6"
B.
clo.

28'-0"
24'-0"
W
h
GARAGE 23'-4" x 23'-4"

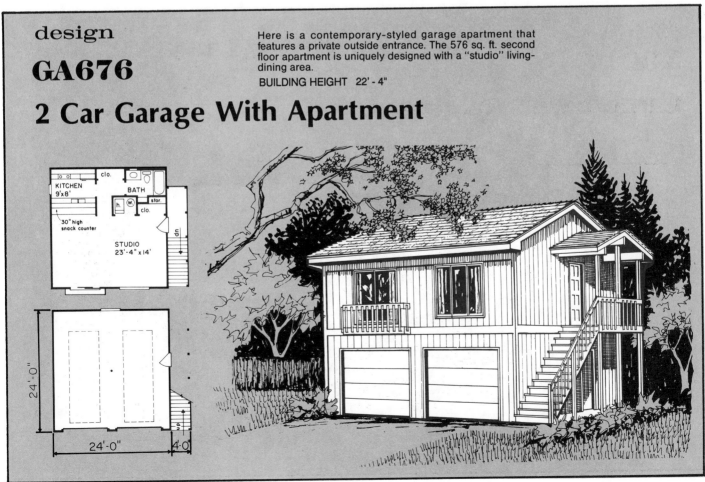

design

GA676

Here is a contemporary-styled garage apartment that features a private outside entrance. The 576 sq. ft. second floor apartment is uniquely designed with a "studio" living-dining area.
BUILDING HEIGHT 22'-4"

2 Car Garage With Apartment

clo.
KITCHEN 9' x 8'
BATH
stor.
h W clo.
30" high snack counter
STUDIO 23'-4" x 14'
dn

24'-0"
24'-0"
4'-0"

design

GA677

This well designed Cape Cod garage apartment will become a welcome addition to your property with the extra income it will provide. The studio apartment is well designed, and the two attractive front dormers add a colonial touch to the building.

BUILDING HEIGHT 22'-0"

2 Car Garage With Apartment / Loft

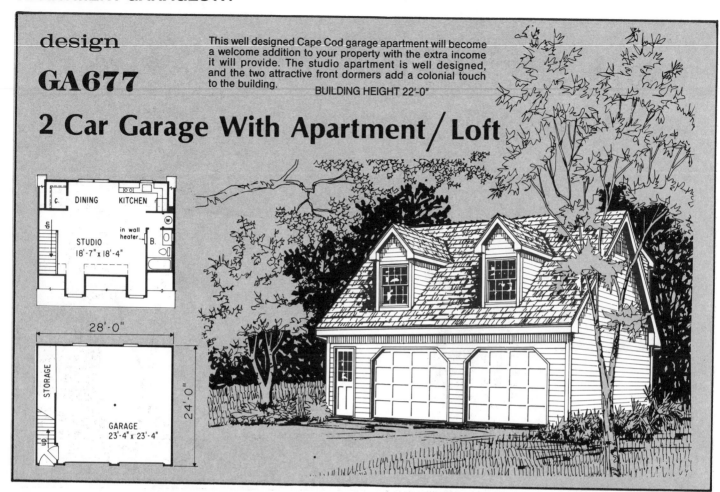

design

X6017

Now, here is something quite unique! This carport/apartment can also double as a vacation hide-a-way. The carport features plenty of room for 2 cars and a boat. The 6' wide deck extending the whole length of the building provides ample space for deck chairs, lounging mats, snack tables, sun umbrellas, etc.

Carport with Apartment

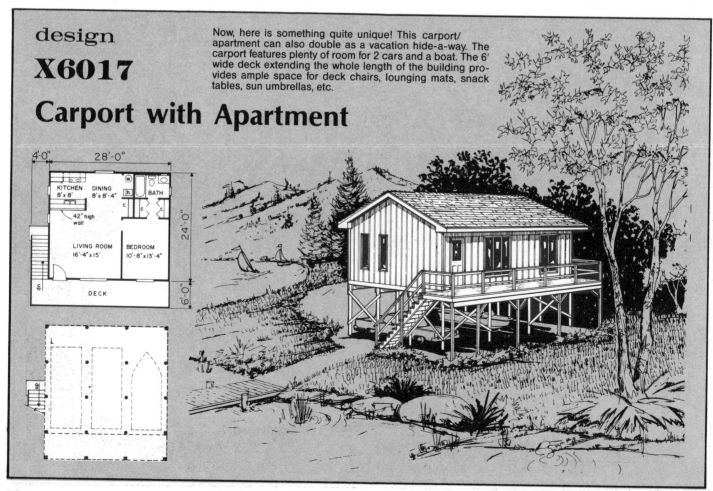

design
P 3018
1½ CAR GARAGE
WESTERN STYLE

This 1½ car garage is especially designed in the contemporary western style. It's 24″ exposed overhang adds charm to the design. There is plenty of space for storage and workbench. Easy-to-follow blueprints include seismic/hurricane construction details.

design
P 3019
2 CAR GARAGE
WESTERN STYLE

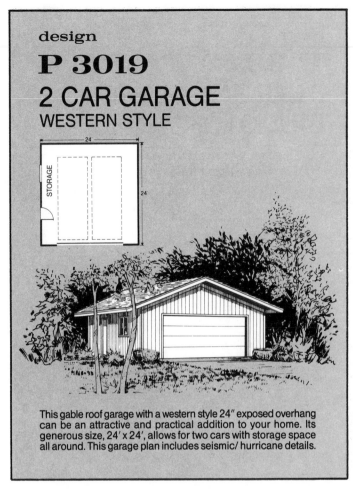

This gable roof garage with a western style 24″ exposed overhang can be an attractive and practical addition to your home. Its generous size, 24′ x 24′, allows for two cars with storage space all around. This garage plan includes seismic/ hurricane details.

design
P 3020
2½ CAR GARAGE
WESTERN STYLE

Designed to fit western home styles. The attractive 24″ roof overhang gives needed protection for the overhead doors. Construction plans include seismic/hurricane details. This functional 30′ x 24′ garage will house two cars and provide the extra storage space most people need.

design
P 3021
ECONOMY SIZE 3 CAR GARAGE

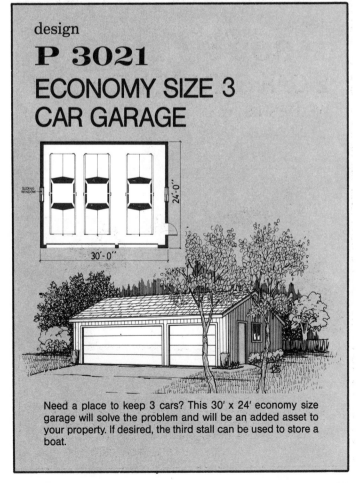

Need a place to keep 3 cars? This 30′ x 24′ economy size garage will solve the problem and will be an added asset to your property. If desired, the third stall can be used to store a boat.

design
P 3022
3 CAR GARAGE WITH STUDIO LOFT WESTERN STYLE

Large studio loft 32' x 16'

BUILDING HEIGHT 21'-4"

More than just a garage! This 3 car garage features a loft that can be used as a studio or office... features that many homeowners are looking for. This 32' x 24' garage is designed in the contemporary western style. Easy-to-follow blueprints include seismic/hurricane construction details.

design
P 3023
2 CAR GARAGE
WESTERN STYLE

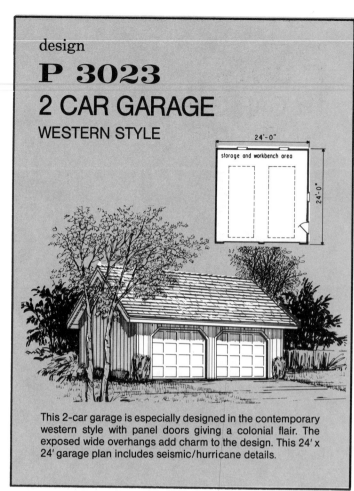

This 2-car garage is especially designed in the contemporary western style with panel doors giving a colonial flair. The exposed wide overhangs add charm to the design. This 24' x 24' garage plan includes seismic/hurricane details.

design
P 3024
2 CAR GARAGE WITH LOFT
WESTERN STYLE

Designed to fit the contemporary western home style, with attractive 24' exposed overhangs, this 2 car garage has a 26' x 12' loft area. It can make a good hide-a-way studio or just plain storage space. This garage plan includes seismic/hurricane details.

BUILDING HEIGHT 21'-0"

design
664
2 CAR GARAGE WITH LOFT

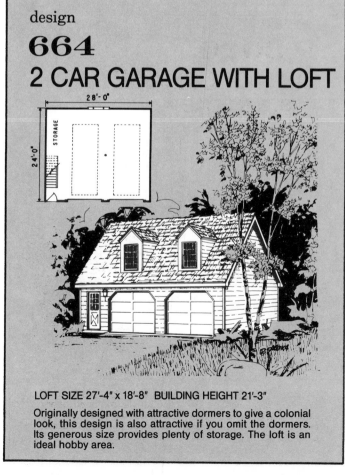

LOFT SIZE 27'-4" x 18'-8" BUILDING HEIGHT 21'-3"

Originally designed with attractive dormers to give a colonial look, this design is also attractive if you omit the dormers. Its generous size provides plenty of storage. The loft is an ideal hobby area.

FOR NOTES AND LAYOUT PROCEDURES

SCALE ¼" = 1'-0" PER SQUARE

FOR NOTES AND LAYOUT PROCEDURES

SCALE ¼" = 1'-O" PER SQUARE

UCANDO® PROJECT PLANS

All plans are easy-to-follow and fully detailed. A complete list of material included.

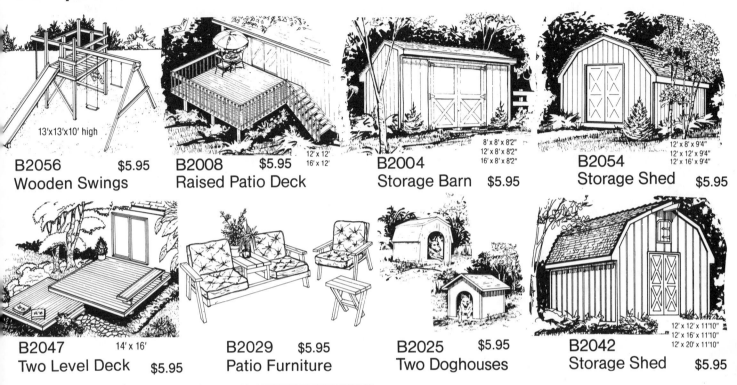

B2056 $5.95
Wooden Swings
13'x13'x10' high

B2008 $5.95
Raised Patio Deck
12' x 12'
16' x 12'

B2004
Storage Barn $5.95
8' x 8' x 8'2"
12' x 8' x 8'2"
16' x 8' x 8'2"

B2054
Storage Shed $5.95
12' x 8' x 9'4"
12' x 12' x 9'4"
12' x 16' x 9'4"

B2047
Two Level Deck $5.95
14' x 16'

B2029 $5.95
Patio Furniture

B2025 $5.95
Two Doghouses

B2042
Storage Shed $5.95
12' x 12' x 11'10"
12' x 16' x 11'10"
12' x 20' x 11'10"

BLUEPRINT ORDER FORM

- When you're ready to order construction blueprints we recommend that you order them from the dealer who provided this book.
- Your dealer can give you valuable and cost-saving information about local building code requirements and the availability of local contractors and financing should you so require.
- Take advantage of your dealer's knowledge and experience!

NATIONAL PLAN SERVICE,INC.
435 WEST FULLERTON AVENUE
ELMHURST, ILLINOIS 60126-9963
PHONE (708) - 833 - 0640

NPS

ALL PRICES SUBJECT TO
CHANGE WITHOUT NOTICE
NOT RETURNABLE

In CANADA Make check payable to
THE LODER COMPANY LTD
14536 115th Avenue
Edmonton Alberta Canada T5M 3P6

PLEASE RUSH ME THE ITEMS CHECKED BELOW

☐ B2040	$5.95	☐ P2005	$7.95	☐ P2016	$7.95	☐ P3003	$7.95	☐ X6006	$12.95	☐ 655	$7.95	☐ 673	$7.95
☐ B2052	$5.95	☐ P2006	$7.95	☐ P2017	$7.95	☐ P3018	$7.95	☐ X6013	$12.95	☐ 657	$7.95	☐ 679	$7.95
☐ B50065	$5.95	☐ P2007	$7.95	☐ P2018	$7.95	☐ P3019	$7.95	☐ X6017	$12.95	☐ 659	$7.95		
☐ B50396	$5.95	☐ P2010	$7.95	☐ P2024	$7.95	☐ P3020	$7.95			☐ 660	$7.95		
		☐ P2011	$7.95	☐ P2026	$7.95	☐ P3021	$7.95	☐ 633	$7.95	☐ 663	$7.95		
☐ GA674	$12.95	☐ P2012	$7.95	☐ P2027	$7.95	☐ P3022	$7.95	☐ 638	$7.95	☐ 664	$7.95		
☐ GA675	$12.95	☐ P2013	$7.95	☐ P2501	$7.95	☐ P3023	$7.95	☐ 642	$7.95	☐ 669	$7.95		
☐ GA676	$12.95	☐ P2014	$7.95	☐ P3001	$7.95	☐ P3024	$7.95	☐ 643	$7.95	☐ 670	$7.95		
☐ GA677	$12.95	☐ P2015	$7.95	☐ P3002	$7.95			☐ 648	$7.95	☐ 671	$7.95		
										☐ 672	$7.95		

☐ Payment is enclosed (check or money order)
☐ Please charge to my credit card below

SALES TAX Illinois Residents please add 6 3/4% sales tax.
AL,CA,MD,OH,WA,TN,andPA Please add appropriate sales tax.
USE CREDIT CARDS ONLY FOR $10.00 OR MORE - U.S. ONLY

☐ VISA
☐ MasterCard

If you wish to use your charge card, check box at left and fill out boxes below.
Expiration Date
Month/Year_____
Credit Card No._____

TOTAL . . . $_____
TAX (see tax note) . . . $_____
Shipping and Handling charges . . . $ **2.00**_____
TOTAL ORDER . . . $_____

Name_____
Address_____
City_____ State_____ Zip_____
Phone ( )_____

NATIONAL PLAN SERVICE,INC.
435 WEST FULLERTON AVENUE
ELMHURST, ILLINOIS 60126-9963
PHONE (708) - 833 - 0640

NPS

ALL PRICES SUBJECT TO
CHANGE WITHOUT NOTICE
NOT RETURNABLE

In CANADA Make check payable to
THE LODER COMPANY LTD
14536 115th Avenue
Edmonton Alberta Canada T5M 3P6

PLEASE RUSH ME THE ITEMS CHECKED BELOW

☐ B2040	$5.95	☐ P2005	$7.95	☐ P2016	$7.95	☐ P3003	$7.95	☐ X6006	$12.95	☐ 655	$7.95	☐ 673	$7.95
☐ B2052	$5.95	☐ P2006	$7.95	☐ P2017	$7.95	☐ P3018	$7.95	☐ X6013	$12.95	☐ 657	$7.95	☐ 679	$7.95
☐ B50065	$5.95	☐ P2007	$7.95	☐ P2018	$7.95	☐ P3019	$7.95	☐ X6017	$12.95	☐ 659	$7.95		
☐ B50396	$5.95	☐ P2010	$7.95	☐ P2024	$7.95	☐ P3020	$7.95			☐ 660	$7.95		
		☐ P2011	$7.95	☐ P2026	$7.95	☐ P3021	$7.95	☐ 633	$7.95	☐ 663	$7.95		
☐ GA674	$12.95	☐ P2012	$7.95	☐ P2027	$7.95	☐ P3022	$7.95	☐ 638	$7.95	☐ 664	$7.95		
☐ GA675	$12.95	☐ P2013	$7.95	☐ P2501	$7.95	☐ P3023	$7.95	☐ 642	$7.95	☐ 669	$7.95		
☐ GA676	$12.95	☐ P2014	$7.95	☐ P3001	$7.95	☐ P3024	$7.95	☐ 643	$7.95	☐ 670	$7.95		
☐ GA677	$12.95	☐ P2015	$7.95	☐ P3002	$7.95			☐ 648	$7.95	☐ 671	$7.95		
										☐ 672	$7.95		

☐ Payment is enclosed (check or money order)
☐ Please charge to my credit card below

SALES TAX Illinois Residents please add 6 3/4% sales tax.
AL,CA,MD,OH,WA,TN,andPA Please add appropriate sales tax.
USE CREDIT CARDS ONLY FOR $10.00 OR MORE - U.S. ONLY

☐ VISA
☐ MasterCard

If you wish to use your charge card, check box at left and fill out boxes below.
Expiration Date
Month/Year_____
Credit Card No._____

TOTAL . . . $_____
TAX (see tax note) . . . $_____
Shipping and Handling charges . . . $ **2.00**_____
TOTAL ORDER . . . $_____

Name_____
Address_____
City_____ State_____ Zip_____
Phone ( )_____